TO
FIND
AN
IMAGE

TO FIND AN IMAGE

Black Films
From Uncle Tom to Super Fly

by James P. Murray

The Bobbs-Merrill Company, Inc.
INDIANAPOLIS/NEW YORK

74-22295

Published by the Bobbs-Merrill Company, Inc.
Indianapolis   New York

ISBN 0-672-51745-0
Library of Congress catalog card number 73-3781
Designed by Paula Wiener
Manufactured in the United States of America
First printing

The author wishes to thank Mike Veny, Linda Carter, Diane Weathers, Laura Harris-Hurd, and Joan Morgan for their suggestions concerning the manuscript during its early stages, as well as Jean Bond and Walter Myers for their encouragement and varied assistance.

Contents

Foreword

We've been there since the start, you know. From the beginning. Black people have been making films in the United States of America (God shed his grace on) since 1917, perhaps before. A movie called *Spyin' the Spy* was produced that year by an outfit called the Ebony Corporation. The film was a reflection of what black life was like then. And the folks were into cowboys and gangsters and relentlessly middle-class value systems . . . and the beauty of maintaining style and reality all through the twentieth century.

Films tell us we have been beautiful people and foolish people, unwise and profound people, blues vagabonds and post-office aristocrats. But we need not be ashamed of anything we are or have ever been—flesh and blood, slave, and quasi-free. All very human things. Films of the past will help to tell us what the future can or cannot be . . . should or should not be. We need them, then. Look at the black films of the teens, twenties (Anita Bush in *The Crimson Skill*), thirties, forties, on down to our own time and place. Look at Robeson, Lawrence Chennault, Slick Chester, others and others. From them we know how we looked and sounded. History. Legend and myth. That's America. Why not us?

The most negative black films of the past were not *made* by blacks. We must remember that. Putting the image of black Americans into the hands of other Americans is like asking management to paint a flattering portrait of workers on strike.

A black film industry in our time is not only a clear possibility but a vital necessity. The correlation between image and destiny now affects black Americans profoundly. We must present a picture of ourselves to prevent our future from being shaped by others—particularly by those to whom our story is either unclear or unpleasant.

That black films can make money has been clear since the days of the great movie entrepreneur, Oscar Michaux. Black films can also define both what life in Black America has been and, hopefully, what it will be.

CLAYTON RILEY

Introduction

Why Black Cinema?

Two questions that must be asked in any book dealing with black cinema are: Is the medium important enough to warrant serious discussion, and is a *black* cinema needed, desired, or practical? To examine the importance of cinema, we must view it historically, within the context of both the American experience and the black experience. Essentially, what any medium does is present an image, musical, visual, or literal, reflecting what people think of themselves in relation to the world. No matter how creative the concept, it cannot be distinct from its socio-historical place.

In the United States, cinema has gone a long way in projecting a kind of beautiful sterility. It has presented images to people who wanted desperately to believe in the American dream of unbridled opportunity and in the possibility of wealth, splendor, and freedom from unhappiness. The early Hollywood offerings were particularly successful, because the films usually depicted situations wherein the success or failure of the hero was determined, not by his force of character, but by the role. Thus, the tall cowboy in the white hat always outdrew the one in the black hat; no good girl ever lost to a bad girl, and we all knew that after the fadeout, sexual activity culminated in simultaneous and ecstatic orgasms.

A more subtle but equally potent projection was the stereotype of successful (therefore worthwhile) people. The man was tall, white, handsome, and self-assured. The woman was small, white, lovely, and self-assured, although often a bit naive. Almost everyone was wealthy. No woman went to the bathroom except to change her makeup.

Hollywood became the creator of folk heroes. The United States, a country too young to have traditional folk heroes, created instant celluloid giants. And most Americans believed in these images. They worried about which "star" was doing what, what so-and-so was wearing, or whom so-and-so was being seen with. This is what America was all about: the ideal. It is necessary to examine the effect of this kind of propaganda rather than its objective merit. For although we may say that Hollywood was producing "unreality," the effect on the country in terms of image and life style was, and still is, very real. Little girls grew up wanting to be Shirley Temple, and those who did look like Shirley Temple were valued more than their plain sisters. Similarly, little boys who were handsome, tough, self-assured were valued more than little boys who were not. When Veronica Lake wore her hair in a certain style, women all over the country did the same and felt more a part of the culture.

Films reflect not only the aspirations of individuals, but also those of society as a whole. The concept of manliness was more important to the "serious" business of life than that of womanliness. Whites were the good guys; Indians, the bad guys; Orientals, the cooks and valets. During the Second World War, most stewards serving on ships in the U.S. Navy were either blacks or Orientals. Not necessarily because these people made better stewards, but because they fulfilled the proper image.

What was the movie industry doing for black people in this country? It was telling them the same things it was telling whites during the thirties and forties: that whites were the important people, the more valued people, and the people on whose side were such notables as God and Cecil B. DeMille. It told black children that white skin was beautiful. And that blue eyes and straight blond hair were beautiful. It was clear that a black-skinned, kinky-haired girl with dark eyes could not be beautiful. And so blacks went to drugstores and beauty parlors and straightened their hair and bleached their skin and accepted, in frighteningly large measure, the value of a white physical appearance. But a more devastating element of what Hollywood was producing was the custom of excluding blacks from the majority of films. The fact that blacks did not exist in the film world contributed more toward their denigration than anything else. It was whites, not blacks, who were significant.

There were some films, however, depicting blacks in a detrimental way. Blacks were shown as cowardly, subservient, obsequious, lazy. These pictures did more to reinforce the attitudes of whites than they did to injure the self-image of blacks. For blacks could no more identify with the shallow creatures on the screen than could whites with badly drawn white characters. The picture of Tarzan beating off fifty Africans prompted black children to identify with the white hero rather than the Africans.

Undoubtedly, movies will continue to exert a strong influence on the way people think of themselves. As techniques evolve, more and more people will be drawn into visual media, if for no other reason than its facility in reaching audiences. The chances are great that visual media will play an increasingly important role in direct education as well. Since the media exert such influence, and because they have historically excluded blacks to the detriment of the black image, blacks, if they are to rectify this omission, should use the media to create their own versions of society. And, to some degree, this is what is happening today.

In discussing black-oriented cinema, it would be more accurate to define cinema as "black" when all aspects, including financing, distribution, and advertising, are black-controlled. However, I choose to call "black" any cinema in which blacks exert significant influence, either by direct input (such as writing the screenplay, starring in, producing, or directing the film) or by indirect participation (such as accepting roles in which no creative involvement is permitted, but in which a black theme has a decided effect.)

The three goals of black cinema are: correction of white distortions, the reflection of black reality, and (as a propagandizing tool) the creation of a positive black image. The majority of black pictures will probably be primarily reactive until blacks can gain full control of their productions. This is because so far it remains easier to get funding for a picture that sharply delineates whites and blacks than for one that minimizes their differences or ignores whites altogether. A picture featuring a black-white clash in which the blacks defeat a very mediocre corps of whites does not offend whites because of the mediocrity of the white actors (or their roles) and because the film points out that blacks and whites are, essentially, at odds. If, at the same time, blacks can be made to look somehow despicable, so much the better. Thus, certain movies will continue to show the "good" black guy as a pimp or involved in drug trafficking and the like. The reactive film, responding to the oppression that blacks feel in the everyday world, does little to alter the black image but is still superior to a Tarzan singlehandedly chasing hundreds of Africans away from Jane.

The concept of black reality divorced from the American dream, which had never been real to either black or white Americans, is the most promising aspect of black cinema. But black reality in cinema will still depend for some time on what white backers see as that reality.

The use of film as a medium for propaganda should not be overlooked. Directed toward both blacks and whites, it holds a promise of understanding that books have not delivered. The visual images of blacks, brought into white living rooms on the six o'clock news, first informed the white public of black anger and resentment. These same images may one day alert whites to the fact that the struggle for existence in the United States is a broader, more profound experience than they imagine.

TO
FIND
AN
IMAGE

1

Movies and Life
and Black People

In June 1972 a crowd sat in a large, dark theater on 42nd Street between Seventh and Eighth avenues in New York City. It was three o'clock on a Wednesday afternoon, and only about thirty of the four-hundred-odd seats were filled. The audience was mostly men sneaking away from work or the world or simply men with nothing to do. Some had apparently been bored to sleep.

This was movie watching, U.S.A.—a pastime, an escape from reality; ostensibly a way to be entertained. Sleepily or otherwise, all eyes were riveted on the huge screen down front.

About halfway back in the middle section of the main floor, a young mother—a black woman—sat with her two children. The boy, no older than five, squirmed in his seat by her side. She held the infant in her arms. Approximately an hour into a second-run movie called *Halls of Anger,* the baby started crying loudly. As if on cue, the son grabbed his distracted mother's arm and tried to gain her attention by conversing loudly.

1

Such scenes were not altogether rare at low-admission 42nd Street matinees; still, many in the audience were visibly annoyed and turned in their seats to stare silently and register their displeasure. Why had this black woman come all the way downtown (they assumed she was from Harlem) to a movie house in the middle of the week with her two children? How could she have expected the kids to sit quietly through a three-hour double feature?

Fundamentally, these questions reflect what most observers fail to realize—that movies have become the greatest sociological influence on black people other than their immediate environment. Not only is the search for entertainment a factor in their lives, but movies are also a way for black people to see themselves in relation to society as a whole.

Since the earliest days of motion pictures, Americans have responded enthusiastically to cinema. Never before had a medium—a mass medium—been able so effectively to take its audiences into past and future fantasies, exotic and forbidden locales, suspenseful and exciting intrigues. Generation after generation, spectators have been stumbling out of theaters weakened by incessant laughter, emptied by profuse weeping, inspired, gratified—even relieved—that the right people had once more triumphed over seemingly overwhelming obstacles.

And statistics indicated that black Americans have long enjoyed movies as a popular form of entertainment, spending proportionately more time in front of the big screen than their white counterparts. As could be exemplified by the young black mother, the reasons are numerous and significant.

The downtown theater itself was one stimulus. Away

from the neighborhood with its trademarked ugliness and problems, the movie house presented elegant, more often garish and superficial, surroundings where even candy bore prestige prices, and stylish people came and mingled with anyone who could afford the price of admission.

Traditional stage plays, even with their closeness to live performers, were no substitute. Even as television came within reach of even welfare families, films remained a means of escape with more atmosphere for black audiences. They could leave their homes for a few hours and, at the movies, become involved more with the world outside their limited environment than they could anywhere else. The theater beckoned to them to come in and feel free to become involved with whoever starred in whatever story. With lush nightclubs, country clubs, and world excursions far beyond their means, where else could blacks see—if not experience—the American dream?

For years, black audiences identified with heroes in Hollywood films—heroes who were invariably white. Black children playing cowboy in front of tenement buildings wanted to be Alan Ladd, Gary Cooper, and John Wayne. Their fathers dreamed of relationships with Mae West, Marilyn Monroe, and Raquel Welch. Black women envisioned estates with luxurious mansions and scores of servants as the real and finest way to live. And of course there were blatant and obvious manifestations of this yearning to identify with whites. Processed hair styles, bleached blond hair, and the use of skin brighteners were attempts to copy the style, appearance, and mannerisms of screen heroes and heroines.

Possession of these superficial "keys" to a fantasy kingdom made the sight of the real world more jarring. The same old ugliness, inequity, and racism in society were still there, and the combination had a cumulative effect. As the black viewer felt compelled to return to the theater (often alone the second time) to see a particular film or performer, his dependence on film to escape society became even more significant.

From the beginning, filmmakers ignored black audiences as such. For although there were blacks in the earliest major films, they were not cast as heroes or heroines. They were not characters black audiences would relate to, much less identify with and emulate. They were often portrayed humorously, and while some blacks laughed, others were outraged.

A combination of forces brought a change. By the late 1960s, most blacks had given up hope that they would ever be absorbed into a color-blind society, and a phenomenon called "race consciousness" spawned the phrase, "I'm black and proud." The message was simple enough: only frustration resulted from blacks identifying with white heroes. Black America wanted (and was willing to pay for) its own heroes.

Astute businessmen that they were, leaders of the film industry translated some of their more popular (and financially successful) heroes and stories into "blackenized" versions that capitalized on carefully research changing attitudes, and these also became popular (and financially successful).

The humble servants, happy domestics, and energetic singers and dancers of an earlier generation were no longer in vogue. Instead, proper gentlemen and professionals able to move about in their chosen fields and take care of business became more popular.

Because it proved more profitable, Hollywood allowed its black heroes to take on and (usually) to overwhelm white society. Black private eyes, policemen, cowboys, and even politicians were permitted to win; however, they still reflected a white view of black experience. This development was followed by a series of "relevant" films, supposedly reflecting the new black militancy. These soon merged into a collection of offensive images, with the emphasis on hustlers, charlatans, dope pushers, and numbers runners, whose token swipes at The Man and society did not minimize their crimes against the black people on the screen and those in theater audiences.

This type of movie did not satisfy the black community, and reports from Hollywood and around the country, from inside and outside the industry, indicated the need for an independent black-controlled cinema network. The concern and reaction were not new. Pioneers in the black community had begun to protest decades earlier, after realizing—as would their future counterparts—that if relevant, meaningful films were to be made, they would have to be made by independent black filmmakers.

Besides fulfilling the creative needs of black artists and the entertainment needs of black audiences, the films would be instrumental in reversing years of propaganda from an industry that had managed to exploit black performers and black audiences for fifty years. The proposed effort would also retrieve millions of misused box office dollars and place them at the disposal of talented black filmmakers. All the planned new activity, the subject of heated discussion in 1972, would be impressive when it happened, but no more important than the work of black pioneers who started with less and still succeeded in making their mark in the black community.

Moving pictures were the last word in entertainment when they caught international attention in the late nineteenth century. In 1895, when Edison in America, the Lumières in France, and Paul in England projected moving pictures onto white sheets, the world thought it a revelation. Inventors worked feverishly at perfecting the art, and by 1900, a French magician named Georges Méliès had already experimented with a new form: narrative film.

Sixteen years later, leaders of the relatively new National Association for the Advancement of Colored People organized in one of the first efforts by blacks to produce a film. Angered by D. W. Griffith's *The Birth of a Nation,* they specifically hoped to make a film refuting the many flagrant caricatures of blacks in Griffith's production. After much discussion, the NAACP decided to earmark funds for lawsuits to halt showings of the film throughout the country.

In 1916, E. J. Scott, Booker T. Washington's secretary at Tuskegee Institute, forged ahead with the idea of a black rebuttal to *The Birth of a Nation.* The initial approach would have added a prologue to the already three-hour-long Griffith film, but Washington and Scott decided to make their own film. Elaine Stern, a professional writer, composed a script entitled *Lincoln's Dream,* a prophecy of black peace and progress. Universal Studios rejected the idea, and Scott used his contacts in the National Negro Business League to raise funds from the black middle class through the sale of thousands of dollars' worth of stock.

It took three years for Scott to finish the twelve-reel *The*

Birth of a Race, shooting in nearby Florida and in Chicago. He was forced to seek white backers to complete his film, and they demanded (and got) major changes in the story and in the organization of the company.

The finished film was a combination of pathetic contrasts: beautiful sets next to visible backdrops and live battle scenes intercut with cheap and obvious stock footage. The original theme of *The Birth of a Race* was lost, and the project could only be termed a failure. Still, it was a failure that taught important lessons. Black producers had learned about runaway shooting costs, about unattainable production goals, and about the importance of avoiding control by white backers.

By the late 1920s, there were some seven hundred movie houses in the black communities of America. They were not the picture palaces of downtown, but in these theaters black audiences were not restricted to balcony seating arrangements. They were also free to enjoy the work of black filmmakers. While these auditoriums were the main centers for the target audience, optional showings at schools, churches, tent revivals, and even once a week at white theaters provided substantial capital to hard-pressed black producers.

At least thirty black film-production companies were operating in the early days of film. Ebony Films, in Chicago, made one-reel parodies of popular stories of the day, beginning with *A Black Sherlock Holmes.* Gate City Film Corporation, the first black film company in the Midwest, opened in Kansas City. In 1922 the noted actor Leigh Whipper formed the Renaissance Company to produce all-black newsreels. Famous Artists made similar films for the black vaudeville circuits in 1927.

Also in 1927, the Colored Players Film Corporation
opened its Temple Studios in Philadelphia, hoping to create a black Hollywood just outside the nation's capital.
Their first film, *Scar of Shame*, still exists in the American
Film Institute archives. It is the story of a young pianist
who rescues a poor working-class girl from the evils of her
environment, marries her out of pity, and then realizes
that he is unable to accept her as one of his class. The
girl is never allowed to meet her mother-in-law, who lives
in a private home with her own black butler.

Scar of Shame dealt with the intraracial prejudice of
the period. Even black-owned film companies chose
actors according to a caste system based on color, a con-
vention blacks, too, accepted in the twenties and thirties.
Light-skinned blacks got the best parts—romantic leads
and good guys. Darker blacks won the more subservient
roles, and also turned up as villains.

Many prominent black actors and actresses, who spent
the majority of their time working in Hollywood, returned
to New York for their summer vacations, during which
they often worked in hastily produced black films. When
these actors—for example, Clarence Muse, Mantan Moreland, and Rex Ingram—came east, they worked for people
like Oscar Michaux, the most famous and successful early
black filmmaker. During a thirty-year period beginning
in 1918, Michaux wrote, directed, produced, and distributed forty-four films, including twenty-four features,
from an office on Harlem's 135th Street. Michaux's career
spanned the silent and sound eras.

As an all-around entrepreneur, Michaux had his own
solution to the problem of distribution. Each spring, he
would tour the theaters of the nation, stopping in town

after town to show movie house managers his new scripts and pictures of his new actors and actresses. Sometimes he brought the players themselves. Then he would barter with the managers for an advance against the films' receipts. By late spring, he would be back in New York City with his production money, and shoot the film in two or three months over the summer, sometimes becoming cameraman as well as director and producer. Michaux would edit his film almost as hurriedly as it had been shot. By fall, he would be off again in his car, distributing and promoting the new production as he went along. The following spring, he would begin again with a new script.

And the system was successful. Even with limited, generally low-income audiences, he was able to make a feature film every year for two decades without a grant, subsidy, or monopoly, an achievement subsequent filmmakers would envy.

While technical excellence was absent from most of Michaux's productions, *Body and Soul,* starring former athlete Paul Robeson at the beginning of Robeson's singing and acting career, proved an artistic triumph. Robeson plays a seemingly venal black preacher living a double life. The preacher shows up in a speakeasy full of criminals and cardsharpers, and then is seen attempting to dupe a pious mother into marrying off her daughter. Near the end of the film, both roles are revealed as shams. Robeson is shown to be a kind-hearted man who ultimately closes the speakeasy. A strong and masculine black image emerged from *Body and Soul,* towering above the stereotypes prevalent in other films of the era.

Most of Michaux's films dealt with race problems from his perspective as a black man. In *God's Step-Children,* light-skinned Naomi falls in love with her handsome step-brother but is forced to marry a dark-skinned repulsive but rich farmer. She commits suicide in the end. The film was an attempt to deal with what seemed an obsession with shades of skin color on the part of some blacks.

Actor Lorenzo Tucker, known in his heyday as the "Black Valentino," said of Michaux, "He didn't lean toward comedy and didn't go much for dialect. Most of the starring roles were gangsters or doctors. Even in his day, Mr. Michaux dealt with the black struggle from a point of view directed at the inner problems."

Carol Mahon, another New York-based actor who appeared in Michaux's films, added, "In a way, he directed with a heavy hand, and, regardless of the play or script, he would always have an upbeat scene with singing and dancing."

Obviously having enjoyed the opportunity to work for a black director, Mahon remembered, "Blacks were misused by whites in films. You were just never given a chance to use your full potential."

Both actors recalled that they were usually paid ten dollars a day as lead players or stars, while screen extras or bit players in Hollywood were earning twenty-five dollars a day.

As the producer who first cast Paul Robeson in a film, and as the first director to make an all-black talkie, *The Exile*, Oscar Michaux made notable contributions in independent black films. He also pioneered in that he floated stocks and bonds in his film enterprises, proving he was a progressive businessman as well.

Like Michaux, most early black filmmakers were concerned with turning out their products on a regular basis and with satisfying the tastes of black audiences. For obvious reasons, technical quality could not be an overwhelming concern. Hollywood was already a source of competition, but black filmmakers found white independents who dealt exclusively with black subjects even more of a threat to the black film industry.

Eugene O'Neill's play, *The Emperor Jones*, was produced in 1933 by John Krimsky, Gifford Cochran, and Dudley Murphy, three white men who believed it would make money as a film. Paul Robeson, now an experienced actor, re-created his stage role—the arrogant pullman porter, who through sheer nerve, becomes king of Haiti.

The Emperor Jones was the first film about blacks to spark serious critical evaluation. Reviews (including those of black newspaper critics) were divided, but nearly all were complimentary to Paul Robeson. Some reviewers believed that the film was significant because a white character had been presented on the screen as the "lackey" of a black, Brutus Jones, and as his intellectual and social inferior. Others attached no great importance to that aspect of the film.

Thomas R. Cripps, a film historian, wrote about commercial response to the film: "The most striking instance of white awakening to the box office power of black themes was *Emperor Jones* . . . which did surprising business and helped persuade Hollywood to re-examine its racial policies. Shot on a low budget in Astoria, Long Island, the picture grossed an amazing $10,000 in one Harlem week. But even more astonishing was the $11,000 it made in Washington, D.C."

While the Colored Players Film Company, Michaux, and other black companies were attempting honest portrayals of black culture and experience, many newer films of the thirties were commercial projects aimed at black neighborhood theaters: westerns, detective stories, and romances written, produced, and directed by whites in black locales with black actors. These films were cheaply made, but the circumstances were different. Their producers were financially able to do better, yet they turned out B-plot pictures with titles like *Bronze Buckaroo, Dirty Gerty From Harlem,* and *Murder on Lenox Avenue.*

Jack and Bert Goldberg, founders of a company called Negro Marches On, made all-black films for ten years and were typical of (if more successful than) most white producers of black-cast films.

In a 1942 interview, the Goldbergs described their films candidly. "We don't go in a great deal for star names, because a colored performer who's a great hit up North may not mean a thing to our audiences south of the Mason-Dixon line. All they know is that they want plenty of singing and dancing or drama depicting Negro life in typical Negro spirit. They are wonderful audiences, too; there's nothing sophisticated or cold about them—but they definitely know what they want."

In these condescending remarks was the essence of exploitation. However, the Goldbergs were apparently not as money-oriented as other white producers; in fact, they initiated a plan that allowed talented students from predominantly black Tuskegee and Hampton institutes and Howard University to work and learn at their studios. These students received fair wages for the time: $100 a week for principals, $60 a week for supporting actors. But the Goldbergs understood that the key to the movie business was distribution, and they carefully appraised and mapped out their audience—thirteen million American blacks in about five hundred theaters, plus those at midnight performances in southern white theaters.

"Personally," Jack commented, "we're crazy about our colored associates. We find them willing, eager, accomplished, and always gay. There's never a downcast moment when a Negro film is in production. No temperament either, and no petty jealousies."

A typical Goldberg production was the quickie western, *Bronze Buckaroo,* produced in 1938. Bob Blake, a tall, handsome black man with a white Stetson, silver spurs, and a pearl-handled pistol, rides up to the ranch of pretty Betty Jackson, whose father has been shot. Action builds to a standard shoot-out in Mesa Canyon, and Bob and Betty ride off into the hills as his sidekick and other pals look on.

The Goldbergs never hired white actors and apparently had no urge to do so, but they did use professional white technicians. For example, Arthur Lenard, one of their regular directors, was a Warner Brothers veteran.

As more companies joined the competition, some themes were obviously influenced by or were imaginative interpretations of newspaper headlines. In the Louis Weiss production, *Drums O'Voodoo,* black voodoo practitioners and witch doctors form an alliance with Roman Catholics against some diabolic villains. In *The Black King,* a deacon organizes a Back to Africa movement, taking advantage of ordinary blacks. His army marches to New York, but there the fleece game falls apart, and the self-styled "Emperor of the United States of Africa," once gaudily uniformed and imperious, must hike back to Mississippi as a hobo.

The works of the Goldberg brothers, Ted Toddy, and

other white independent filmmakers who capitalized on the black market were purely commercial and inherently exploitative. Ted Toddy, president of Toddy Pictures, was quoted in 1947: "Negro audiences do not care for the heavy emotional dramas. Their choice in film entertainment is the picture which features light comedy, outdoor adventures, musical comedies with an abundance of singing and dancing, and comedy-romances." It was such self-assurance on the part of white filmmakers like Toddy, who took black audiences for granted and felt qualified to speak on their needs and desires, that especially infuriated black filmmakers and artists.

There were several reasons for the decline of the black film circuits in the late forties. Theaters had always been marginal enterprises, and economic downturns in the forties and fifties hurt their business. Most theaters were owned by whites, who were operating strictly for the money. When profits dropped and part of the black audience was lost to television, they simply closed their doors. At the same time, Hollywood began its own appeal to black audiences. These factors squeezed both black and white independents out of the market.

Nevertheless, for thirty years they had kept before the black people of America a vision of dignity and reality sometimes tinged with humor, which, while often technically poor, was never seen in Hollywood films.

By the end of World War I the American film industry dominated the world market. For movie maker and movie fan alike, all roads led to Hollywood, the big-time center of fame and fortune. At the turn of the twenties, filmmaking was also a big business, the newest industry in the United States. Studio stocks began to be listed on Wall

Street and, in 1919, to be handled by respected firms like J. P. Morgan and Kuhn, Loeb.

The decade of the thirties was the most important in the history of American cinema. In that era between world wars, which included a depression, society underwent great changes that were mirrored in its films. It was a decade called the "Golden Age," with stars like Harlow and Cagney, directors like Howard Hawks and John Ford, and producers like Sam Goldwyn. It was also significant for the growth of talkies.

Once sound and music had been integrated into films, Hollywood began importing black dancers, singers, and musicians, who were overflowing the New York theaters and nightclubs. Their talents were recruited for the "all colored, all singing, all dancing" Hollywood epics of the thirties.

Back in 1915, *The Birth of a Nation,* directed by a man many considered to be the first major American director, was released. It took audiences by storm. Twelve reels long (almost three hours), with a special score performed by a full symphony orchestra, it swept along with a cumulative force that has perhaps diminished over the years. Still, there had never been a film like it before; "like writing history in lightning," Woodrow Wilson described it. The passions it aroused and the tensions it created were not forgotten outside the theater. Patrons overflowed the streets, and race riots and mob action followed its presentation in many cities.

In New York the film was banned for some time, and it was also refused license for exhibition in Connecticut, Illinois, Kansas, Massachusetts, Minnesota, New Jersey,

Ohio, Wisconsin, and other states. Indignation was to continue for years.

The Birth of a Nation was D. W. Griffith's epic drama of the sensitive period in American history that began before the Civil War and continued through the Reconstruction era. Besides vividly depicting the horror of the Ku Klux Klan, the film pictured Civil War and Reconstruction blacks as devoted, humble servants or bestial, evil threats to American society.

And blacks were not the only ones outraged by the film. In his book, *The Rise of the American Film*, historian Lewis Jacobs said of *The Birth of a Nation*:

The film was a passionate and persuasive avowal of the inferiority of the Negro. In viewpoint it was, surely, narrow and prejudiced. Griffith's southern upbringing made him completely sympathetic toward author Thomas Dixon's exaggerated ideas, and the fire of his convictions gave the film a rude strength. At one point in the picture, a title bluntly editorialized that the South must be made 'safe' for the whites. The entire portrayal of Reconstruction days showed the Negro, when freed from his white domination, as an ignorant lustful villain. Negro congressmen were pictured drinking heavily, coarsely reclining in Congress with bare feet upon their desks, lustfully ogling the white women in the balcony. Gus, the Negro servant, is depicted as a renegade when he joins the emancipated Negroes. His advances on Flora, the 'Little Colonel's' sister, and Silas Lynch's proposal to the politician Stoneman's daughter are overdrawn to make the Negro appear obnoxious and audacious. The Negro servants who remain with the Camerons, the dignified southern white family, on the other hand, are treated with patronizing regard for their faithfulness, and the necessity of the separation of Negro from white, with the white as the ruler, is passionately maintained throughout the film. The social implications of this celebrated picture aroused a storm of protest in the North.

Actually, black stereotyping and caricatures have been traced back through American theater and filmmaking to as early as 1893. Typical of those objectionable films was *The Wooing and Wedding of a Coon,* in 1905, described by the producers as "genuine Ethiopian comedy." Like the Rastus Films series and a string of Sambo comedies, all depicted blacks as clowns with minimal intelligence. Interestingly, most of these idiot roles were effectively acted by whites in blackface.

In Hollywood, the so-called "pioneer black film" was Twentieth Century-Fox's 1929 production of *Hearts in Dixie.* That story of an old black man's sacrifices for his son was in circulation during the same period as Metro-Goldwyn-Mayer's *Hallelujah,* directed by King Vidor. *Hallelujah* was about a country man who is momentarily charmed by an evil woman. Some of the trademark contrivances in the two films were musical numbers, spirituals, prayer meetings, and even some cotton-picking. They spurred the sensitive, crusading Paul Robeson to write a critical article reacting to both films in *Film Weekly.*

But other black faces were to appear in a series of films by W. W. "Woody" Van Dyke II of M-G-M, beginning with *Tarzan, The Ape Man* in 1932, the first of many African films shot in studio jungles—with studio "Africans."

By the mid-thirties, two performers named Stepin Fetchit and Bill Robinson were becoming increasingly popular with movie audiences. Fetchit, who was to become the first black film millionaire, made up to $10,000 a week at the height of his thirteen-year career on screen. At one point, he had six horses, a fleet of limousines (including a pink Cadillac with his name inscribed on the side), and a retinue of Chinese servants. By 1944 his living style had forced him into bankruptcy.

In 1936 Margaret Mitchell's novel *Gone with the Wind* was published, and in less than three years United Artists had begun a film version.

The film was a success far beyond expectations and continued to draw appreciative audiences thirty years after it was initially released. Actress Hattie McDaniel, the "Mammy" of heroine Scarlett O'Hara, became the first black film artist to be nominated for an Academy Award (as best supporting actress). Not everyone who saw her in the film was so approving, and the NAACP and other pressure groups sought to eliminate more offensive aspects of the characterizations by Miss McDaniel and another black actress, Butterfly McQueen.

In 1937 director Mervyn Leroy used the medium to condemn southern lynch laws. Clinton Rosemond played a black janitor accused of murdering a white high school girl in *They Won't Forget*. The film featured Claude Rains as an ambitious lawyer attempting to defend the accused man, and Lana Turner in her first screen role. The Warner Brothers production, more significant for its attack on racism than its portrayal of blacks, was nevertheless a landmark.

But *They Won't Forget* was an exception to the rule. Most film subjects in the thirties—westerns, historical and literary epics, horror tales, and musicals—offered little opportunity for blacks aspiring to serious screen roles. Another notable departure from the norm occurred in 1940 with the classic film *The Biscuit Eater,* which was filmed in Georgia. One sequence, a dream passage, features a young black child who joins a white youngster, and they venture into a swamp to search for a lost bird dog.

Cabin in the Sky, a landmark musical featuring an all-black cast, was produced two years later. Vincente Minnelli, who was considered the finest musical director of his time, developed the popular musical that pleased wartime audiences with its often fantastic elements. Black religion was the main theme. The film depicted a black heaven and hell in the milieu of a slum in the Deep South. Eddie "Rochester" Anderson, Lena Horne, and Ethel Waters starred in the highly acclaimed film. Noting the success of the revivalist theme, Minnelli worked a special number, "Jericho," into *I Dood It,* a Red Skelton comedy produced the following year. In one scene, Hazel Scott rehearses a number backstage with a group of black singers gradually working themselves into a revivalistic frenzy.

Not surprisingly, there were a number of similar all-black musicals like *Stormy Weather, Thank Your Lucky Stars,* and *Jammin' the Blues.* Talent was abundant as Bill Robinson, Fats Waller, Count Basie, Duke Ellington, Cab Calloway, Louis "Satchmo" Armstrong, and Katherine Dunham appeared.

But black intellectuals were still dissatisfied with the image of blacks in musicals and other films in which they had roles. In 1944, Lawrence Reddick compiled a comprehensive list of damaging black stereotypes perpetuated by feature films: savage African; happy slave; devoted servant; corrupt politician; irresponsible citizen; petty thief; social delinquent; vicious criminal; sexual superman; superior athlete; unhappy non-white; born cook; born musician; perfect entertainer; superstitious church-goer; chicken and watermelon eater; razor and knife toter; uninhibited expressionist, and mental inferior.

While these images did not improve significantly for another thirty years, during the period of 1946-49 social consciousness—occasionally evident in the thirties in films like *They Won't Forget*—reappeared. Suddenly, "problem" pictures with race prejudice themes were being made.

Twentieth Century-Fox was the leader in this genre with such films as *Pinky,* a drama featuring Jeanne Crain as a light-skinned black girl who returns to the South after passing for white in a Boston nursing school. The film had racial stereotypes on both sides of the color line but was redeemed by a forcefully dramatic court scene with a decision in favor of the heroine. As the mother of Miss Crain, Ethel Waters gave one of her strongest performances.

Stanley Kramer's *Home of the Brave* began what was called the "Negro cycle" of 1949. James Edwards played a black serviceman, crippled, amnesiac, and in shock after a reconnaissance mission to a Japanese-held island. A psychiatrist learns that Edwards's best friend, killed during the mission, had called Edwards a "nigger," and so precipitated his mental and physical crisis. The film and its black star won wide acclaim.

Clarence Brown went to William Faulkner's home town of Oxford, Mississippi to film *Intruder in the Dust,* based on the Faulkner novel about a stubborn black man jailed for shooting a white man in the back. Juano Hernandez played the lead, with only fourteen other actors in the cast. Five hundred local residents enthusiastically joined the professionals and added an air of reality to the film. Shooting on location and using local residents were new to the industry at that time, and one of those responsible for this new development was Louis de Rochemont.

Like all de Rochemont's films, *Lost Boundaries* was based on a real-life story. This one was about a boy whose light-skinned father had passed as white and practiced medicine for twenty years in New Hampshire. In the film the father (played by Mel Ferrer) renounces his race to pursue his career. Although it followed the pattern of earlier films by black producers, blacks felt *Lost Boundaries* was dishonest and unrealistic, since pressure for the doctor to cross the color line came in reality from whites, not blacks, as the film implied. And as in the case of *Pinky,* light-complexioned black actors and actresses were overlooked when the lead roles were cast.

Lost Boundaries was banned in Atlanta as "likely to have an adverse effect on the peace, morals and good order of the city," and the ban was upheld by the Fifth Circuit Court of Appeals.

Black actors appeared in scores of other Hollywood films in the forties and played the familiar (but damaging) roles, such as train porters and domestics.

Hollywood in its first three decades was unkind to black actors and unconcerned about black audiences. The smiling, happy faces on the screen reinforced the impression that Hollywood represented an artificial world set up in the daytime and dismantled at night. For black audiences and actors, the happy ending wasn't really happy at all. And yet it took years to realize how much damage had been done.

2

The Black Actor

What is the role of the black actor or actress? To define it we must first look at the problem all black artists face: What roles are allowed? We would be remiss in advising the black actor to accept only roles that fit his definition of black reality. We would be saying he should rule against his own livelihood. A fairer suggestion would be that the black actor refuse roles that are demeaning to blacks and try to make those he does accept conform to standards of intelligence, dignity, and race consciousness. Reviving the Stepin Fetchit type of character would be objectionable to audiences today, but playing a sensual hero might be acceptable if the other qualities in the character's personality were attractive enough for emphasis and added dimension.

An actor who is judged on his performance in what is basically a white-controlled picture must be judged with reservations. White control cannot justify playing roles damaging to blacks, but allowances should be made for the restrictions on an actor's interpretation of his part.

Another consideration is: Who is allowed to become a

film star? The preference for ex-athletes over established black actors in order to cater to the box office gives us a limited pool of talent, sensitivity, and professionalism to draw upon. If Jim Brown is selected for a role over Paul Winfield because Brown is judged to be a popular draw, it is doubtful that we see an inspired acting talent. The judgment that an athlete would exercise in choosing roles is likely to be less discriminating because he is aware that his entertainment career will be based more on his physical appeal than on his acting qualifications. While a superstud role may flatter the athlete, the established actor has to consider whether it will actually injure his career. It will surely be pointed out by some white critics that these problems exist in the white cinematic industry as well, but only the most biased and callous will fail to recognize the difference between incidence and totality involved.

In 1950, *Home of the Brave* toured the nation's theaters, and James Edwards's powerful performance earned him *Jet* magazine's designation as the first black dramatic film star. But competition swiftly followed. Later that year, a newcomer, Sidney Poitier, was seen in his first feature film.

Two singers made their reputations as film actors in the fifties. One was a calypso crooner named Harry Belafonte; the other, a stage brat with years of entertainment experience, named Sammy Davis, Jr.

Belafonte came to New York, tried the stage, and then turned to singing, specializing in vibrant and exciting island music. His interest in acting continued, however, and in 1953, he appeared with Dorothy Dandridge in *Bright Road*, which dealt with the problems of a black youth. Philip Hepburn played the troubled boy. It was prime material for sensitive and engrossing treatment, but the character's anxieties were only superficially explored.

The following year, Belafonte appeared with Miss Dandridge in a black operetta, *Carmen Jones.* Oscar Hammerstein's musical drama set in the Deep South was a successful modernization of Bizet's tragic and passionate opera. Miss Dandridge played the lustful heroine and Belafonte her chief victim. They were backed by a cast that included Pearl Bailey, Diahann Carroll and Roy Glenn.

The island of Barbados was the locale for *Island in the Sun,* released in 1957, with Dorothy Dandridge and Belafonte co-starring again. This tale of two interracial couples was based on a novel by Alec Waugh. Though the film's story was somewhat confusing, it provided a new setting for a once forbidden theme.

Belafonte starred in two films in 1959. He gave a first-rate performance in the melodrama *Odds Against Tomorrow* as a young singer in conflict with a southern drifter. New York location scenes were skillfully shot, and the cops-and-robbers scenario by black novelist John O. Killens was excellent.

His second project was *The World, the Flesh and the Devil.* Belafonte played one of three survivors left on earth after a devastation by a radioactive salt. When he is joined by Inger Stevens and Jose Ferrer, the initial suspense falters, but the film offered fascinating moments of science fiction.

Sammy Davis, Jr. credits Frank Sinatra with helping him break into films. In the fifties, Davis and Sinatra, Dean Martin, Joey Bishop, and Peter Lawford were known around Hollywood as the "clan." A film in which they collectively starred was *Oceans 11,* the story of a holdup attempt in Las Vegas.

Davis did not restrict himself to "clan" films. In *Anna Lucasta* (1959), Davis portrayed a jive-talking, finger-snapping sailor just off the boat who meets a good-hearted, seemingly reformed prostitute played by Eartha Kitt. Like a couple of other black films of the era, it was adapted from a successful Broadway play. The film suffered from contrived dialogue and predictable action.

Davis was one of an all-black cast in the screen adaptation of George Gershwin's *Porgy and Bess,* another black vehicle borrowed from the New York stage. Davis gave a memorable performance as the flashy Sportin' Life. The folk opera of black life in a South Carolina slum followed *Carmen Jones* as the second black musical of the decade and proved that the Hollywood formula was still viable.

As Belafonte and Davis became popular in the late fifties, James Edwards was seen in dramatic roles in *The Phoenix City Story* (1955), *Tarzan's Fight for Life* (1958), as well as in *The Joe Louis Story, Steel Helmet, The Manchurian Candidate,* and *Night Is A Quarter Moon.*

Other less well known black performers appeared occasionally in films of the fifties. Juanita Moore was the grief-stricken black mother whose daughter, Susan Kohner, passes for white in *Imitation of Life.* (Gospel singer Mahalia Jackson sings when Miss Moore dies in the film.) Frank Silvera played a police lieutenant in *Crime and Punishment, U.S.A.* Canada Lee was seen in *Cry, the Beloved Country.* Pearl Bailey sang in *That Certain Feeling.* Louis Armstrong appeared in *Glory Alley, The Five*

Pennies, and *Paris Blues.* Even Stepin Fetchit was back
(with Jimmy Stewart in the 1952 western, *Bend of the
River*), but unfortunately it was in a role reminiscent of
earlier decades.

Clifton MacKlin appeared in *The Mark of the Hawk,*
a drama that explored racism in South Africa. Sidney
Poitier co-starred, and was also in the 1957 production
Something of Value, about Kenya's struggle against white
supremacy. Paralleling the white-Indian conflicts in
North America, colonization leads to violence. Poitier
played a black whose friendship with a white man in the
tense environment is tested. In the fifties, Poitier was developing as an actor, and would win an Academy Award
nomination before the decade ended.

3

Sidney Poitier, The Black Superstar, Finally Arrives

Sidney Poitier was approaching the second decade of his film career, and he was a superstar in every sense of the Hollywood definition. In 1968 the motion picture distributors voted him the nation's number one box office attraction. He had been nominated for the Oscar for his brilliant acting in *The Defiant Ones* (1958), and five years later had won the Academy Award for his role in *Lilies of the Field*.

In 1950 Poitier had made his first feature film, *No Way Out*, with Richard Widmark and Stephen McNally. He starred as a black doctor barely tolerated by whites in a metropolitan hospital. A psychopath nearly sparks a racial conflagration following the death of a relative who was one of Poitier's patients. Poitier brought a cool dignity to this role.

At forty-four, Poitier had started his own production company, and in 1972 was a partner with Barbra Streisand, Steve McQueen, and Paul Newman in a consortium called First Artists Productions. He planned to set his own film schedule, appearing regularly as an actor. He announced that he was also considering more directing and producing, and possibly retirement.

During his more than twenty years on the screen, Poitier had portrayed a high school youth in *Blackboard Jungle*, a musician in *Paris Blues*, a Moorish warrior in *The Long Ships*, and a frustrated young husband in *A Raisin in the Sun*. He made important contributions as a black artist in some of these roles.

In 1967, *Guess Who's Coming to Dinner* had a familiar plot, but was still a commercial success, partly because of an idealistic concept and story twists (including an interracial marriage ultimately approved by both sets of reluctant parents). The following year, Poitier starred with Abbey Lincoln in *For Love of Ivy*, the first black screen romance.

Also in 1969, Poitier filmed *The Lost Man* in Philadelphia, playing a black militant who organizes a robbery to get funds for a ghetto program and then dies in the arms of his white girlfriend. Local residents were used in the picture.

Poitier's estimated gross income in 1968 was $9 million. He had by then starred in twenty-five movies and four plays. *Guess Who's Coming to Dinner* was being shown at the same time as *In the Heat of the Night* and *To Sir with Love*, a low-budget box office success shot in London. These three were Poitier's most commercially successful films. By 1971 they had grossed over $55.6 million in the United States and Canada alone.

Shrewd business sense was partly responsible for

Poitier's rapid rise to wealth. His gamble—lower salaries and a percentage of the profits—paid off handsomely.

Until recently, if asked to name all the black actors he knew, the man in the street—black or white—might have remembered few besides Sidney Poitier. As the black representative in films, and in the effort to be all things to all people, the tension and pressure on Poitier were great. He had to visit a New York psychiatrist four times a week for four years. Only in the late 1960s did the pressure diminish.

Poitier talked to Chester Higgins for a 1969 *Jet* article. "It is a relief. You'll never know how lonely those years were for me when I was the only black star out there. Now I walk down the street and see Jim Brown's name big on the marquees, and I feel good. I'm not just a token black representative any more. Now I feel like I'm just one of the fellows out there. . . . With the appearance of people like Jim Brown and Raymond St. Jacques, Ossie Davis and Ivan Dixon and Calvin Lockhart, I can walk around like a peacock these days.

"You know, when a picture of mine didn't make money before, there were always those in the industry to say, 'Well, those guys (meaning black, but they would never have to use that word) just aren't commercial.' That's why so many before me—Rex Ingram, Canada Lee, others —didn't get a real shot at film stardom. At the moment, I'm just kind of pleased that the film industry has finally begun to recognize that Poitier is only one of many black actors and actresses who can do interesting things, artistically and commercially, who can enhance the film industry on the artistic and commercial basis."

In his position of high visibility, Poitier could not avoid

criticism. A *New York Times* article, "Why Does White America Love Sidney Poitier So?" by black playwright Clifford Mason, discussed "what makes for a proud image and what makes for a demeaning one."

He said, "It is a schizophrenic flight from identity and historical fact that anybody can imagine, even for a moment, that the Negro is best served by being a black version of the man in the gray flannel suit, taking on white problems and a white man's sense of what's wrong with the world. I, too, am tired of *Porgy and Bess*. But at least it doesn't try to fool us. Even though its Negroes are frankly stereotypes, at least we have a man, a real man, fighting for his woman, willing to follow her into the great unknown, the big city, poor boy from Catfish Row that he is.

"What did we have in *The Bedford Incident* by comparison? Poitier is a black correspondent who went around calling everyone sir. Did anyone see Gary Cooper or Greg Peck call anyone sir when they played foreign correspondents? In *Duel at Diablo* he [Poitier] did little more than hold James Garner's hat—and this after he had won the Academy Award. What white romantic actor would take a part like that? He gets to kill a few Indians, but James Garner gets the girl and does all the real fighting. Poitier was simply dressed up in a fancy suit, with a cigar stuck in his mouth and a new felt hat on his head."

Sidney Poitier, the undereducated Bahamian boy—who once slept under newspapers on New York roofs; who was kicked out of the American Negro Theater because his West Indian accent made his colleagues laugh; who bought a fourteen-dollar radio, listened to it every night for six months and imitated the sounds; who appeared in an Army Signal Corps documentary in 1949, and made only $7,500 in his first commercial movie—was a success, but was lacking a screen identity.

William Marshall, a black actor better known for his Shakespearean theatrical roles than for his film performances, commented to *Soul*: "Poitier, like many other prominent black men, is carrying the cross for all of us without having anything to say about it. I personally feel that he's far more talented than Gregory Peck or many other big actors and should be recognized for his talent, but in these times his 'Negroness' dominates his being."

Aware of the criticism and concern about his screen image, Poitier had this explanation for the drabness of the characters he played: "It is because the guys who write these parts are white guys, more than not; they are guys in a business and they are subject to the values of the society they live in.

"And there are producers to deal with who are also white. And a studio with a board of directors, also white. So they have to make him—the Negro—kind of a neuter, and it has to be avant-garde, which is easy, right? You put him in a shirt and tie and give him a white collar job, then you can eliminate the core of the man: his sexuality. His sexuality is neutralized in the writing. But it's not intentional; it's institutional. To think of the American Negro male in romantic social-sexual circumstances is difficult, you know. The reasons are legion, and too many to go into."

In 1972 Poitier returned to the screen in *Brother John*. For the third time, actress Beverly Todd co-starred, this time as his romantic interest. Poitier portrayed a superhero. As in *In the Heat of the Night*, the locale was a small southern town, and the conflict (between an intellectually superior Poitier and the bigoted local sheriff) was resolved with Poitier as the winner. Some critics said Poitier's hero progression had spun off to a pompous extreme. One reviewer thought *Brother John* presented the actor in a quasi-ethereal role that transcended any resemblance to reality. But to many black audiences, a "brother" was winning and that was good enough.

Hollywood actors often become fascinated with the other side of the camera. Many have attempted to make the transition from actor to director; some successfully, others not. *Buck and the Preacher* was a co-production of Poitier's E & R Productions and Belafonte Enterprises. It was the teaming of a pair who had been friends for twenty-six years. But the project ran into problems. In the first week of shooting, "artistic differences" arose between Poitier and the film's director, Joseph Sargent, also an old friend and classmate from the Drama Workshop of the New School of Social Research.

When it was all over, Poitier himself had taken over the direction. The company was on location at Durango, and there were other rumors, such as reports that Mexican actors were complaining of underpayment and discriminatory hiring. The film rapidly became the subject of conversation in Hollywood, but on location the deposed director minimized reports of problems.

"The man had breathed and lived it since its conception," Sargent explained to *Variety*, referring to the screenplay. "No one knew the material better than he did. He should be the man to put it on the screen. In no way would it work with another director. . . . It's his film. It's as simple as that, and there was nothing racial about it whatsoever."

But co-star Belafonte said, "If the nature of the subject wasn't working and dealing as deeply as it did with the black psyche, it might not matter."

Buck and the Preacher was the story of a wagon train of ex-slaves heading west to homesteads after the Civil War. As in *The Lost Man* and *Brother John,* half the production personnel, stuntmen, and cast were black. In addition, there were six minority group trainees, including an Indian and a Mexican-American who had been brought from the States with the rest of the crew. One of them—Drake Walker, an apprentice director—had written the original story on which *Buck and the Preacher* was based.

On location for *Buck,* Poitier gave his unit publicist, Walter Burrell, a wide-ranging interview that later appeared in *Soul.*

"I have an attitude now which allows me to function and enjoy life," he said. "And I will continue to make the kind of films I want to make. Some of them are going to fail. Some of them are going to be bad pictures, but I am accustomed to not winning all the time. Losing doesn't damage my ego. I slide right by a loss looking for another win. If I spend too much time brooding over a loss, then I don't have time to grow.

"You may have noticed—and this is the first time I've mentioned this—that when I get jumped on for a bad movie, you never hear a peep out of me. You never hear any refutations, no placing the blame somewhere else, no discussion how bad the director was, no discussing the other actors, no complaints that the writer didn't do a good script. The next time around, if it's a great success, you still won't hear one damn peep out of me. That's the way I live."

About the black movement, he said, "And one thing I truly believe is that we will have made a major step forward when we stop trying to tell other folks how to be black. We're all going toward the same philosophical place. We've simply got to accept the fact that there are many roads leading there—and be tolerant of those traveling those other roads."

With the footage from *Buck* finished and under firm control, Poitier maintained his active pace, going on to San Francisco to do *The Organization,* a Mirisch Brothers production released by United Artists. It was to be the last of three "Tibbs" detective pictures, and it quickly became a boxoffice hit.

Between takes for the crime movie, Poitier worked on the editing of *Buck* in the Francis Ford Coppola Studio, released by Columbia in the spring of 1972.

While *The Organization* was circulating as well as rumors of a sequel to the unreleased *Buck and the Preacher,* Poitier went to London where *A Warm December* was filmed in the spring. It was his first film for First Artists Productions, and was produced by Poitier's Verdon Cedric Production Company. Until filming actually began, Poitier's decision to direct his second film was a well-guarded secret. *A Warm December* was the first English-located film under National General's global distribution pact with FAP.

During this period, *Buck and the Preacher* was finally released; it had been previewed eight months earlier. The film was an immediate box office success despite mixed critical reaction.

On May 1, only weeks after the film opened, Poitier and Belafonte appeared as the sole guests on "The Dick Cavett Show." They had come to promote the film, and although Poitier admittedly was uncomfortable in a talk show environment, a rather unusual thing happened: The two artists explained that during the filming (with its attendant problems), the company had honored a special request, permitting George Goodman, Jr., a writer and editor for *Look*, to spend a week on location researching a story about the film.

What appeared in the magazine, three months after the visit, they described on national television as "poor journalism." For an entire segment of the show, Poitier and Belafonte took control of the interview to criticize the magazine (to which they had previously written indignant letters) and its black writer. Goodman, they felt, had devoted more time to describing the supposed animosities of the two leads and to recording bits of juicy and unsubstantiated gossip than he had to describing a major production effort.

4

Diahann Carroll and Female Singers Take the Lead

Black artists, out of the necessity for survival, are often stimulated into a variety of endeavors. A number of black actresses began, and often continue, to double as nightclub and concert singers. Pearl Bailey, Lena Horne, and Eartha Kitt were pioneers in this respect, but Ethel Waters is still popular in the gospel field, and was even invited to the White House by President Nixon in 1971.

More recently, Diahann Carroll, Abbey Lincoln, and relative newcomers Barbara McNair, Lola Falana, Paula Kelly, Freda Payne, Diana Ross, Dionne Warwick, and Leslie Uggams have appeared in feature films. Established actress Diana Sands also has a musical background, though she is not known as a singer.

Diahann Carroll began her film career in musicals of the fifties, then appeared with Robert Hooks in Otto Preminger's *Hurry Sundown,* and later with Jim Brown in *The Split.* Then she left the screen to star in a television comedy, *Julia.*

36

Barbara McNair, a fair-skinned beauty, made her film debut in *If He Hollers, Let Him Go*. The film was heralded by a *Playboy* photo story of Miss McNair's nude love scene with Raymond St. Jacques. In the film, she plays a nightclub singer whose boyfriend (St. Jacques) is falsely accused of killing a white girl in a southern town.

The familiar theme was not helped by a weak script, and the fact that the film had obviously been shot on the West Coast added to its artificial effect. But beauty, potential, and *Playboy* publicity worked, and soon Miss McNair was seen in *Change of Habit, Stiletto, Venus in Furs,* and *The Lonely Profession*. She co-starred with Sidney Poitier in *They Call Me Mister Tibbs*, and returned to San Francisco with him two years later to re-create the role of his wife in *The Organization*.

In a conversation with a *Soul* reporter about acting, she said, "Well, the woman's place in film—and I'm referring to all women—has been mainly as a love object. That's basically what women are in films. And Hollywood hasn't come to the point where they want to put a black love story on the screen, even though there was a little bit in *If He Hollers*. Somehow, they don't like to see black people making love on the screen. They haven't gotten to the point where they think of black people being in love. They still think of the animal type of sex when it comes to the black image in films."

Sidney Poitier turned writer to develop a tender love story in which he takes an ordinary woman, a domestic worker, glamorizes her, and "spoils her rotten." But despite Poitier's prestige, no major film studio was ready to buy *For Love of Ivy*, and it was finally made by Palomar Pictures. Abbey Lincoln, previously seen in *Nothing but a Man,* was selected for the title role and performed with grace and charm. The film had humor and romance, but was most important for the precedent it set.

Dionne Warwick, a versatile established pop singer, appeared in *The Slaves,* a Deep South story with a twist in the interracial affair between a plantation owner and a black slave woman. The film was not a great success. But it did make money, and its well-researched script dealt openly with slave life and provided an insight into the agony and frustration of the system. In her screen debut, Warwick gave a strong performance as the wretched concubine.

Months later the interracial love theme, again in the Deep South, was updated. Another neophyte, Lola Falana, sultry protégée of Sammy Davis, Jr., appeared as the wife of a black mortician and mistress of a white sheriff in *The Liberation of L. B. Jones.*

Pre-release publicity of the film's explicit love scenes prompted some curious reaction. The film's producer, Ronald Lubin, reported to authorities that telephone callers had threatened to kill him if the film was released. No such threat was carried out, but a fist fight between two agitated theater patrons brought a note of violence to the New York opening. Miss Falana was also featured in a *Playboy* pictorial, but two years after filming, she had, like Miss Warwick, apparently become uninterested in movies.

Movies are a form of communication and a reflection of societal attitudes. For a particular audience, they are a link with home. The American serviceman overseas has letters, newspapers, and periodicals as self-initiated contacts. The military sponsors a newspaper and a radio-television service, and regularly shows Hollywood feature films. *L. B. Jones* was booked into military theaters in Europe. A synopsis in the Army and Air Force Motion Picture Service's program handouts read: "A southern attorney takes on the divorce case of a black mortician whose wife is fooling around with a white policeman; it nearly blows the roof off a small Tennessee town." After being screened in Germany in Frankfurt, Heidelberg, Mannheim, and Wiesbaden, the film was removed from the military circuit in the spring of 1971, nearly a year after it had first been released in the States.

A spokesman for the European Command cited the movie's "inflaming" effect on military race relations, a special problem in an area where perverted race pride under Nazism had reared its ugly head forty years earlier. The EUCOM official said the film appeared to "have a disturbing effect on moviegoers" and "be inflaming to whites and blacks," adding that "the film tended to undermine programs which strive to ease racial tensions and solve racial problems without resort to violence or illegal acts."

In the meantime, pressure for more blacks in film and television continued within and outside the industry. Young women with pretty faces and shapely bodies finally were granted a modicum of the elusive success many of their counterparts had been receiving for decades. It was 1968, and suddenly women like Ena Hartman, Jeanne Buckley, Gloria Calomee, Janee Michelle, Lyn Roman, and Brenda Sykes were seen more often on the screen. Beverly Todd became a favorite of Sidney Poitier's and appeared with him in three films.

But perhaps the most successful of the new starlets was Judy Pace, younger sister of singer-dancer Jean Pace.

Voted by *Daily Variety* "the most beautiful black woman in Hollywood," Miss Pace was made famous as the college coed seductress in *Three in the Attic.* She had begun with parts in *The Candy Web, The Fortune Cookie, Hi in the the Cellar,* and *The Thomas Crown Affair.*

In a major role in *Cotton Comes to Harlem,* she was nude again in a seduction scene. Then she starred in *Up in the Cellar.* Her success was measurable by her salary having doubled every year between 1965 and 1970. Then she co-starred in a television series, "The Young Lawyers," for which she won an NAACP Image Award as Outstanding TV Actress. She returned to the screen in *Brian's Song, Cool Breeze,* and *Frogs* released in 1971 and 1972.

Nat King Cole appeared in *The Cincinnati Kid* and *China Gate,* and later played the role of the minstrel in *Cat Ballou.* His daughter, Carol, after a debut with Dean Martin in *The Silencers,* decided to move to Europe and carry on the family's name in films. She first appeared with Assaf Dayan in *Promise at Dawn.* In a 1970 interview with *Jet,* she took Hollywood studios to task for trying to keep her, as a black actress, in a certain bag. "I had another part in a picture where I was supposed to be kind of a Girl Friday," she explained, "but I actually came on more like a maid. There was a good love-making scene written in, but the head of the studio decided that would never do, this black and white thing. And then they were supposed to kill me at the end of the film, but he thought that would never do, either. They killed a dog instead.

"I know for a while, everywhere I was going for interviews in New York had a slave movie in the mill. Now where's that at?"

At the time of the *Jet* interview, Miss Cole was already a member of the black American expatriate colony in Paris, studying French and planning to act in French films.

In Hollywood there were no black female stars of Sidney Poitier's stature. There were actresses with years of theater experience, like Claudia McNeil, Juanita Moore, Kitty Lester and Beah Richards, and newer stage actresses like Rosalind Cash, Gloria Foster, Janet MacLachlan, Gwen Mitchell, and Cicely Tyson. More were being turned out by New York repertory companies like the Negro Ensemble Company and the Al Fann Theatrical Ensemble.

It was hoped that the lack of meaningful roles for black actresses, which had been a major handicap for so many years, would soon be corrected. But Hollywood's version of black women may not have been what increasingly sophisticated black audiences wanted. It was clear, however, that roles for black actresses would not be greatly improved until comparable roles had been improved for their male counterparts.

5

Jim Brown and Other Saturday Heroes

The varied, indirect routes blacks often take in reaching career success is a familiar topic of discussion. An example often cited is the development of black ministers into powerful politicians or opinion-makers. Adam Clayton Powell is perhaps the best known, but Martin Luther King, Jr., Jesse Jackson, and Rev. Walter E. Fountroy (who was elected a Congressman in 1970) had messages that reached beyond their congregations.

It is so in other fields, and in 1966 the news that the Cleveland Browns' star fullback was leaving at the peak of his career to play the field in Hollywood was greeted with skepticism, although he had already appeared in a film.

Jim Brown had made his acting debut two years earlier in *Rio Conchos,* shot during football's off-season. When the film was released, some doubters had admitted that he might make good. Within five years Brown was an established, often controversial, film star.

Brown's success opened the door for the gridiron professionals who followed after him. After nine seasons and 126 touchdowns, and with the image of a record-setting pro football superstar, he did not lack confidence. As admirers observed him leaving the field, apparently oblivious to the acclaim and adoration of the fans around him, the word went out in excited whispers, "Jim Brown is cool, man."

By 1969 the film goal line had been crossed, first by Woody Strode and Harold Bradley, and later by Rosey Grier, David "Deacon" Jones, Bernie Casey, Tim Brown, Dick Bass, Fred Williamson, and John Amos. O. J. Simpson, who played college football in Hollywood's back yard, made the jump to pro in two areas at once.

The rationale behind the move from the gridiron to the greener grass of Hollywood is that the risks are quite small. Brown was already a hero and sex symbol; his acting ability was of less importance.

Brown brought his quiet self-assurance to Hollywood. Some say he still is not and never will be an "actor." But his performances improved with each film, and soon Hollywood's ingredient for star status—controversy—was added. Between rumors of spats with a girlfriend; a fight with another football player over another girl outside a nightclub; an alleged assault following a fender-bender; and a feud with his co-star, Raquel Welch, attention and audience response increased.

Following *Rio Conchos,* he was in *The Dirty Dozen, Ice Station Zebra, Dark of the Sun, Year of the Cricket, The Riot, The Split,* and *100 Rifles,* his eighth film in three years.

100 Rifles was the film in which he starred opposite Raquel Welch. Love between blacks and whites remains a box office attraction. This film used the theme and starred two popular sex symbols. Publicists tried to play up a sizzling love scene, but soon rumors of a cool off-camera relationship hit the wires. Long lines greeted the film when it opened in city after city. Reviewers attempted to decide which star's performance had been the worst. The public disregarded the critics and went to see *100 Rifles* for the sex and the good old-fashioned western-style fighting.

Over a year passed before Brown acted in a film again. Some industry observers said rumors and bad publicity had begun to take their toll. But when Brown filmed *Slaughter* and *Black Gunn* in quick succession early in 1972, it was evident that he had made peace with the industry as well as with one of his former leading ladies; celebrity watchers saw him with Raquel Welch on several occasions.

Woody Strode headed the seniority list of black ball-carriers in films. While a student at UCLA, he had waited on tables at Warner Brothers in the summer. After short football-playing stints in the forties with the Hollywood Bears, the Los Angeles Rams, and Canada's Calgary Stampeders, he broke into movies as a stuntman.

He graduated to movie and television roles as a Hollywood "African"; a typical film was *Tarzan's Fight for Life*. But his roles improved, and in *Sergeant Rutledge* he portrayed an all-black cavalry unit's first sergeant, accused of assaulting a white woman on the frontier. His dignified performance stood out in an above-average story treatment, but he did not get star billing for playing the title role.

He appeared in films like *Pork Chop Hill* and starred as a gladiator in *Spartacus* and as an archery expert - soldier of fortune in *The Professionals.* In 1970 he had co-star billing as Omar Sharif's companion in *Che.* Other film credits spanned a career of over twenty years, but still he was forced to seek employment in Europe after a ten-year period in Hollywood during which he barely made a living.

Harold Bradley was another early starter, and he was in several productions, filmed primarily in Spain, before returning to the States to teach acting.

Jim Brown was instrumental in getting parts in his films for fellow ex-athletes. Dick Bass of the Rams appeared with Brown in *The Grasshopper.* Bernie Casey, a former teammate of Bass's and a talented graphic artist, began his acting career in *The Guns of the Magnificent Seven* and joined Brown in *tick tick tick.*

Like Brown, many players chose at first to stay in football, appearing in films during the off-season. In 1969, Bass and his teammates, David "Deacon" Jones and Roger Brown, had dual careers.

The anti-military satire, *M*A*S*H*, featured Fred Williamson and several former teammates still with the Kansas City Chiefs in a hilarious football game. The entire Detroit Lions team appeared with Alan Alda in a screen adaptation of George Plimpton's *Paper Lion.* Rosey Grier was in several films, but showed an equal interest in singing and television work.

Although more have been recruited from football, other sports figures have turned to the screen. Professional boxers, including Joe Louis, Archie Moore, Floyd Patterson, and Sugar Ray Robinson have appeared in films.

Tennis star Althea Gibson put aside her racquet for a small role in John Ford's *The Horse Soldiers.*

The Olympic decathlon champion, Rafer Johnson, after having been a West Coast sportscaster, appeared in *Games,* and at one point was being touted as the black Clint Eastwood. (Eastwood had become a high-priced star after starring in a series of low-budget, Italian "spaghetti" westerns.) Johnson appeared in a number of films, including *Soul Soldier.*

The Jackie Robinson Story and *The Joe Louis Story* were among the few black biographical films, although *Go Man Go,* with Sidney Poitier, was about the origin and development of the Harlem Globetrotters.

6

Godfrey Cambridge and Other Funny Men

Blacks in humorous situations have long been popular with American film audiences, and such actors as Willie Best, Stepin Fetchit, and Mantan Moreland kept movie-goers smiling. But not until the 1960s did black comedians receive wide acceptance outside black nightclubs, though their biting satire was aimed at white audiences as well. Godfrey Cambridge's handling of racial humor made it inoffensive to sensitive listeners, and Cambridge became the most successful black comedian to act in films.

He was a hit in the film version of Ossie Davis's *Gone Are the Days (Purlie Victorious),* and had parts in *Bye Bye Braverman, The President's Analyst,* and *The Biggest Bundle of Them All.* He co-starred in *Cotton Comes to Harlem* and played the title role in *Watermelon Man.* Both films had humorous, satirical moments. Relatively successful at the box office, they ushered in a new type of film, aimed chiefly at black audiences.

Standup comic Richard Pryor also turned briefly to films and appeared in *The Busy Body* and *Wild in the*

Streets. His career took off in 1972 after an appearance in *Lady Sings the Blues,* and he had roles in *Wattstax, The Mack* and *The Hit* successively. Bill Cosby, who broke important ground in a dramatic television series, winning three Emmy awards, entered the movie field later than the rest. Redd Foxx was in *Cotton Comes to Harlem* and later starred in a television series, "Sanford and Son." Dick Gregory, the satirist, appeared with blond Diane Varsi in *Sweet Love, Bitter,* distributed as a sexploitation film under the title *It Won't Rub Off, Baby.* His contribution to films was about as important as that of Slappy White, who wound up in a similar exploitation epic.

There were professionally-trained, theater-experienced actors who journeyed to Hollywood from New York and other parts of the country. William Marshall, Raymond St. Jacques, Roscoe Lee Browne, Brock Peters, Robert Hooks, James Earl Jones, Yaphet Kotto, Moses Gunn, and Al Freeman, Jr. were among those who had difficulty finding starring roles, particularly in Hollywood. A few were able to survive in television; others decided to return to the stage; but all held out hope of a brighter day for black actors on the screen.

7

New Social Issues

When Stanley Kramer, perhaps Hollywood's most crusading liberal, produced *Home of the Brave* in 1949, the picture wrung dramatic response from audiences. But the paucity of such crusades became evident in 1958 when he produced *The Defiant Ones,* because the theme still seemed fresh, controversial, and daring.

Hollywood has recognized the honesty of certain themes, including that of black-white relationships. In their own way, filmmakers have dealt with prejudice for decades, but the make-believe world of the screen has generally failed to do much more than entertain.

The provocative questions raised are usually answered with compromise endings. When there is a tragic closing sequence, or no solution is proposed, theatergoers are apt to ignore the "message," discussing character portrayals, favorite scenes, and funny lines, rather than the film's social implications.

With sporadic and often questionable precedents, film efforts to present and update black problems continued through the 1960s, hitting a peak near the end of the decade.

For Paramount, Jules Dassin produced *Uptight,* which probes ghetto reaction after a real-life tragedy, the death of Martin Luther King. The film did not receive unanimous critical acclaim, but it was the first attempt to focus on the dynamics of the severe ghetto confusion and turmoil following the assassination. It focused on the crisis-ridden identity search of a man who turns in a brother; the frustration that leads to militancy and the efforts of moderate community leaders to abate it; the rejection of help from a white liberal sympathizer; and the police-killing of a young black leader. The story bore close resemblance to headlines of those tense days, and black members of theater audiences often responded vocally to what was happening on the screen.

Another film that touched deeply on the minds of a people oppressed was the Italian-made *Battle of Algiers.* This highly influential film about the Algerian rebellion against the French between 1954 and 1957 won eleven international awards, including Best Picture Award at the Venice Film Festival when the film was released in 1966. By intercutting scenes of personal conflict with journalistic coverage of mass movements (such as spectacular fighting sequences), director Gillo Pontecorvo captured the tragic and contemporary drama of private ambivalence in the midst of overwhelming political events. It was a stirring film, and there was talk of militants in the black community, as well as other radicals, taking notes at screenings.

Nothing but a Man, a production by independent filmmakers Michael Roemer and Robert Young, won wide acclaim. It was selected for exhibition at both the 1964 and 1970 New York Film Festivals. Ivan Dixon and Abbey Lincoln starred in this drama about the struggle of a southern black man and his wife in a hostile society. The age-old problems of earning a living, supporting a family, and living in peace and dignity are intensified because the man is black. He refuses to play the expected "Negro" role, despite the warnings of fellow workers, the pleas of his father-in-law, and the tensions in his marriage.

Free of the usual sentimental clichés and blatant messages, *Nothing but a Man* was one of the few films that succeeded in presenting blacks as human beings instead of standard stereotypes. Ivan Dixon and Abbey Lincoln were excellent in the central roles and were supported by a fine cast. The film was a major achievement in black-oriented filmmaking.

Sidney Poitier's *The Lost Man* had similar threads, but the film as a whole was not so effective; his death as a black militant leader was predictable. But in this film, his offscreen role was more important. He succeeded in breaking down racial barriers behind the scenes. For the first time in screen history, the technical crew was nearly fifty percent black. Blacks worked as electricians, production assistants, makeup artists, wardrobe assistants, publicists, tailors, grips, and still photographers. There was a black assistant director. Poitier had gone to each department at Universal, requesting that blacks be given production jobs. He made similar requests when he filmed *They Call Me Mister Tibbs* and *Buck and the Preacher*.

In 1969 (before *The Lost Man* showed Poitier in a new type of part) an outspoken twenty-year-old blond actress from apartheid South Africa said, "Sidney Poitier plays sissy roles. They're actually prissy. Can you imagine being engaged to a man and only kissing him twice? That was *Guess Who's Coming to Dinner*." Genevieve Waite had played the title role in a British-produced film called *Joanna*, memorable for fine photography and an excellent performance by Donald Sutherland. The film used London as the background for an interracial love affair with some of the most explicit black-white lovemaking scenes ever shown until that time.

"The response to the film—and no one can fool me—has been centered around the love scenes between Calvin and me," Miss Waite said. "Calvin" was Calvin Lockhart from Nassau, in the Bahamas, who was effective as a slick, handsome nightclub owner.

Two Gentlemen Sharing, another British-produced import, featured Hal Frederick as a West Indian who travels to London and moves in with a perplexed white roommate after answering an apartment ad. The roommate's girlfriend complicates their uneasy relationship, and the film broadly hints at England's own racial problems.

By the late 1960s, as a tidal wave of black consciousness swept across the nation, some of its effect was felt in Hollywood. Black actors and actresses, always concerned with image, became even more sensitive to the roles they felt should be played. And they were not alone in their concern.

Writer-producer-director Stirling Silliphant, himself at work on a number of black-oriented films, told *Jet* he was fearful that the trend of race pictures was a "dangerous fad." Too many, Silliphant said, portrayed "an unreal, everything-is-right world," while the races were actually involved in serious confrontations. He believed the Negro in Hollywood was trapped between a new "unrealism" and an old "tokenism."

As a screenwriter and producer, Silliphant's attitudes were reflected in his 1967 production *In the Heat of the Night*. It was one of the decade's most powerful films with a black-oriented theme, and the first in a trilogy of Virgil Tibbs roles for Sidney Poitier. Poitier played an expert Philadelphia police detective who solves a murder for an ignorant southern small-town sheriff (Rod Steiger). In the tense drama of cultural and social conflict suspense was effectively balanced by subplots dealing with overt racial prejudice, realistically handled by an excellent supporting cast. Both stars drew critical acclaim. Steiger won an Oscar, and the film was voted four other Academy Awards including Best Picture, Best Writing (screenplay based on material from another medium), Best Film Editing, and Best Sound.

Hollywood has tried repeatedly to visualize black aspirations to be white, beginning in the forties with films like *Pinky* and *Lost Boundaries*. A new attempt was made in 1959 wih *Imitation of Life*, a clumsy production in which a young girl (Susan Kohner) passes and marries into a white society family, endures intense suffering, and finally returns to her black mother with her future unresolved.

Four years later, the screen version of a best-seller reversed the situation. What would it be like for a white man to live temporarily in a black world? The answer was *Black Like Me*. Like the book, the film made its point, but belabored that traditional bugaboo, the sex issue.

Another such effort was the satirical fantasy about a white man who awakens to find he is black. *Watermelon*

Man was a study in frustration with a melancholy ending.

In 1969 *A Change of Mind* had a similar theme. Raymond St. Jacques played the black body in which the brain of a brilliant deceased district attorney is placed. The outlandish plot develops as his wife and colleagues try—but fail—to adjust to the brain's new exterior. A court case with political and racial implications is injected. The film ends with St. Jacques abandoning wife, friends, and career.

Interracial relationships have been tested on the screen with varying results. In 100 *Rifles* (1968) Raquel Welch is gunned down, and Jim Brown leaves town. In *Joanna* (1968) Calvin Lockhart ends up with a jail sentence, and Genevieve Waite pregnant but hoping for his early release. Sidney Poitier and Joanna Shimkus fall to a police barrage in *The Lost Man* (1969). Elizabeth Hartman portrayed a blind girl in love with Poitier in *A Patch of Blue* (1965). They part at the end of the film with the future uncertain. *Guess Who's Coming to Dinner* (1967) had an interracial marriage between Poitier and Katherine Houghton, but the newlyweds leave the country less than twenty-four hours after their marriage.

One black writer to tackle the theme of interracial-sexual relationships was LeRoi Jones. His play, *The Dutchman*, was adapted for the screen in a Reade release starring Al Freeman, Jr. and Shirley Knight. A neurotic white woman picks up a young black man in a New York subway. There is an outpouring of powerfully written dialogue reflecting Jones's view of the racial bitterness and sexual tension that accompany such relationships.

Not much was funny about race relations in America in 1969. A year after the assassination of Martin Luther King,

Jr., a presidential commission had called American society "racist." Black-white confrontations continued in high schools, on the streets, and even in military situations. There was talk of backlash and a backlash to the backlash. Even moderate leaders like the late Whitney Young, Jr. and Roy Wilkins were taking stronger positions.

There had been no recent black-oriented films qualifying as comedy. There were many with a few light moments and a few with many light moments. But blacks were justifiably sensitive about cinematic humor. There were still cries of "stereotype!"—most chuckles in these films were the result of a black's making a fool of himself. And blacks in theater audiences knew that whites were usually laughing, not at an actor or a movie, but at a race.

Nevertheless, a movie called *Putney Swope* was released that year. Advertised as "the truth and soul movie," it was meant to be funny but also to make a statement. Through a fluke, a black man (played by Arnold Johnson) is made head of a Madison Avenue advertising agency. The message was not hard (for whites) to take because it was all a spoof, a put-on, a what-if fairy tale that would end with the last credit. For those looking for a moral, maybe it was that black wasn't so bad after all. The film did have style; it depicted brothers in a loose, casual behavior and pulled few punches. It turned off a lot of viewers—black and white—but it was an education. In selling white products with black commercials, it probably sold itself to success.

Black biographies reappeared. Among the more significant was Ely Landau's Academy award nominee, *King: A Film History From Montgomery to Memphis*. The film traced the work of the late Dr. Martin Luther King, Jr.

from 1955 until his death in Memphis in 1968. All the material was authentic, and much of the 2½ hours of footage had never before been viewed by the public. The film was released in three hundred cities in 1970 to raise funds to continue the civil rights leader's work.

The Great White Hope, a Broadway play based on the career of fighter Jack Johnson, was released as a movie in 1970. James Earl Jones won an Oscar nomination for his portrayal of the title role. A documentary, *Jack Jones,* complete with vintage film, followed a few months later.

Another champion fighter, then on the comeback trail, benefited from a film about his colorful but controversial career. He called himself Muhammed Ali, and he rarely needed an introduction because he was *A.K.A. Cassius Clay. Eldridge Cleaver* was a look at the Panther leader in exile in Algeria, and this was followed by another Oscar nominee, *Malcolm X* (a Warner Brothers release in 1972), at least two documentaries on Angela Davis, one on Bobby Seale, and another on Chicago Panther Fred Hampton.

Hollywood movie makers seemed partial to small-town and southern courthouse locales. *Hurry Sundown; One Potato, Two Potato; To Kill a Mockingbird; If He Hollers, Let Him Go;* and *The Learning Tree* portrayed dramatic cases in small-time courts with clear-cut guilt or innocence established. The question was whether screen justice bore any resemblance to the type meted out in real-life southern courtrooms. Many would be inclined to say not.

One film bypassed the South to examine Middle America. In 1961, *Take a Giant Step* was adapted to the screen from a Louis Peterson play. Johnny Nash, a black pop singer of the period, played an intelligent, sensitive youth growing up in a strained environment, a middle-class white community. Some realistic problems in the story of the youth's confusion over racial prejudice and sex are suggested, but the effect is weak compared with the implied possibilities of the script.

In chronicling a different environment, the ghetto, few films have the power of *The Cool World,* shot in Harlem in the early sixties. Filmmaker Shirley Clarke follows a teenager through a short but significant part of his adolescence. Conflict with parents, an older teen hooked on drugs, love and sex during puberty, hostility as a street gang organizes for a fight, and the obsession of the young boy to own a gun are all vividly shown. The film presents ghetto life in a compelling semi-documentary style.

In 1967, Mrs. Clarke refocused her cameras for another frank insight—this time into the emotions and thoughts of a homosexual who just happens to be black. The cinema-verité camera rolled for twelve hours to capture a day's frustration; the final version runs an hour and forty-five minutes. In *A Portrait of Jason,* Jason is played by the real Jason Holliday (born Aaron Paine, in Trenton, N.J.). He describes his existence and relives his experiences with humor and pathos. The film was bold in its treatment of this controversial sensitive topic, and therefore an obvious shock to some; nevertheless it was realistic and thought-provoking.

In 1965 Columbia released Richard Quine's filmic view of a growing problem—drug addiction. *Synanon* was filmed at Synanon House in Santa Monica, where experiments in saving addicts had begun in 1959. Eartha Kitt and Bernie Hamilton were in the cast. The script was reportedly based on real cases and real Synanon residents. The result showed the dedication of cast and director in trying to dramatize a problem that many didn't understand; few felt it could get worse. Shirley Clarke had also produced a drug film called *The Connection* three years earlier.

We have observed that Hollywood and the independent film establishment, often at the urging of black actors and actresses, showed some awareness of black problems in the fifties and sixties. Some in the industry and viewing public were quick to attack that awareness as tokenism or attempts to use vulnerable subject matter for commercial reasons. Others pointed out that most of the screenplays were unconvincing because their themes and characters were improperly developed.

It was with the players that audiences identified. Music, editing, realistic sets, and props were important, but the performances a director was able to get from the cast were a large measure of his achievement.

Hollywood had played a major role in shaping America's view of its black citizenry. Offering starring parts to athletes and singers was a slap in the face to professional actors and actresses and reinforced the industry's refusal to give the black community unique screen heroes. In essence, Hollywood was saying: We know of your involvement with music and your adoration for sports, Black America. We refuse to glorify your actors and actresses; your sports and music heroes will be your movie heroes too.

For the few actors who were able to show their talents despite the narrow range of roles to which their race had been assigned, artistic freedom was limited by the perceptions of writers and directors. Although black audiences clamored for recognition, the industry allowed only token gestures in their behalf. But black filmmakers were also demanding recognition, and a few writers and directors forged ahead to bring new images to the screen.

In discussing the demeaning roles blacks have played in movies, one must consider not only the performer but also those who controlled the movie. If Stepin Fetchit had been given a choice, his characterizations would have been considerably different. He would no more have demeaned himself than would the white cop in *Cotton Comes to Harlem* if that had been a *white* production. In *Cotton*, the white cop is so anxious to have sex with Judy Pace that he puts a bag over his head when she tells him he is too ugly to face. He looks ridiculous; there was, of course, a black director.

To understand these demeaning roles, we should not evaluate them by what black actors and actresses are doing today, nor by what white counterparts are doing, but rather by what black people have long endured in their everyday living. We too have roles—roles that demean, that hold us back, that leave a bitter taste. When we step out of these roles we often pay a high price. We have been fired from jobs because we stepped out of our roles. We've been humiliated, beaten and lynched. Our homes have been burned, our families attacked.

One thing black cinema can achieve and is already achieving is the neutralization of stereotypes. We used to go from our jobs to watch black women play maids and cooks. We went to movies after our menial, mindless labor to watch black men play menial, mindless roles. Stepin Fetchit, Butterfly McQueen, Bill Robinson, and the black actors in *Birth of a Nation* reflected the reality of the black image to white Americans. What today's actors and actresses are all about, what the vision of true black cinema is all about, is change.

8

Gordon Parks:
Telling His Own Black Story

At age fifty-six, Gordon Parks became the first black director to have a feature film financed and released by a major Hollywood studio. His debut (for Warner Brothers-7 Arts) was an autobiographical screenplay called *The Learning Tree*.

Well-known for his still photography that appeared in *Life* and other magazines, Parks kept an office there while turning his talents to music, writing, and ultimately filmmaking.

In *The Learning Tree,* Kyle Johnson plays young Parks growing up in a small Kansas town in the 1920s. His first sexual encounter, a frustrating love affair, and other experiences of a fourteen-year-old boy living in Cherokee Flats, Kansas are effectively revealed.

Discussing the film before its release, Parks told *Soul,* "It has been heralded by the studio as a tremendously honest film, and they're very excited about it."

Parks was able to make two commercially successful films which were diametrically opposed in temperament and treatment. *The Learning Tree* was a quiet personal memoir. *Shaft* was the opposite and had little of the artistic photography typical of Parks's still camera work so evident in his first motion picture.

In *Shaft,* a black private detective in New York takes on the Mafia and, virtually unaided, prevents a war between an uptown black mob and a downtown white mob. The actions of the hero, Shaft, were patterned after James Bond, but with basic differences. For while James Bond could tear through one violent scene after another without damaging the images of whites (perhaps even reflecting white fantasies more than some would care to admit), Shaft was a more direct representation of the black image. With this in mind, Parks deviated from the original story. In the book, Shaft's girlfriend was a white woman; Parks made her black. The role of the black militant (played by Christopher St. John) was expanded, and a scene where St. John seemingly compromises his position was changed. I asked Parks about these changes.

He said: "There is a uniqueness in having a black director bringing his background to the screen. If I'm successful as a director, others will follow, and we'll have a chance to use our voices. It'll give a new balance to thought in Hollywood where black men have had menial roles for so long. I wanted Shaft to be a hero."

Parks said that Shaft, to be a convincing hero figure, had to be free of ties with whites. His having a white girlfriend would have destroyed the idea of him as distinctly black, tying him emotionally to a situation that most black audiences would find alien. Richard Roundtree, who played the title role in Shaft, was appreciative of Parks's attitude and sensitivity.

"So many black characters in movies are actually extensions of a white man's imagination. This one would have been, too, if it wasn't for the fact that we had a black director." Roundtree expressed the hope that young blacks would find it easier to identify with black screen heroes who were not like the fantasy figures they encountered in white films.

Parks wants to do other films but is determined to accept the dictates of his creative conscience rather than the limitations imposed by the studios. Ten years before making *Shaft*, he was asked by John Cassavetes to assist on a film, but he claims the studio killed the idea because he is black. He had other similar experiences but is nevertheless resisting the temptation—born of frustration—to confine himself to black projects.

In answer to a question about why he made *Shaft*, Parks replied, "I guess a black man has to prove himself, and I've done this picture as an exercise to show them what I can do. . . . And from now on, I want a chance to do the same kinds of pictures that any director does.

"I'm looking all over for projects now," he said, a few weeks after *Shaft* had opened. "I have a hundred scripts in my bedroom now. What I'm not going to do is get myself into the position that requires me to do all black films. I think that would be a detriment to me. It's the same way I worked for *Life* for some twenty years. I never let them push me into a corner to do only black subjects. I try to do everything so it gives me a wider experience and inevitably helps me in all other experiences."

Asked if opportunities for blacks had improved in Hollywood, he replied, "You can't deny that it's getting better. For instance, how can you help but say it's getting

better when *The Learning Tree*, which was absolutely the
first big black film made in Hollywood, was made on the
Warner Brothers lot and was a $3 million production? I
had fourteen or fifteen people behind the camera for the
first time in the history of films. There was a black director.
The producer was black. The scoring was done by a black
man. The third cameraman for the first time was a black
man. This was the first time in the history of motion pictures, and we did our thing. In *Shaft*, we've done the same
thing. The gaffer was black, the wardrobe mistress was
black, the third assistant was black. Isaac Hayes did the
music. Tom McIntosh, who is black, assisted him. We had
two other black guys assisting him. I can name all down
the line. There were black guys in just about every department. And I insisted on this, and M-G-M backed
me up. I was a black American doing a black film in
Hollywood. I don't have to tell you everybody was looking and saying, 'Can he do it?' Hollywood was looking too.
I was taking on the double thing of: Can a black and
white crew mix? I was taking all those chances on my first
picture that nobody ever took before."

How did all this come about?

"It took a strong young man like Kenny Hyman (of
Warner Brothers) to break down all those barriers after
all those years," Parks said. "It took one man to say,
'We're going to have a black director in America; we're
putting up the money. Anything he wants, he has.'

"In *Shaft*," he went on, "it took the courage of Jim
Aubrey and Doug Netter, who were the heads of the
studio out there. There were factions who wanted a white
director for *Shaft*. So when these men, who are heads of
studios, say there will be a black director, it can happen,

and it can happen overnight. If Kenny Hyman had not wanted me, there probably would be no black directors today, because the minute he did it, everybody felt, 'Well, it's happened. We better open up now.'"

He predicted, "There are going to be more black directors now. In the next five years, there's going to be not just Ossie [Davis] and [Melvin] Van Peebles and myself; there are going to be other young black directors all over the place. The only thing I would say to them is: 'Get prepared, because it's going to happen.' It's no longer any use to stand back and say, 'They're not going to give me a break,' because they've done it. How much more do you want? They've got three black directors now. In the next two years, I'll say there's gonna be one or two more black directors."

What about the ever-present problem of studio interference?

"Well, the studio heads will always be there. It's up to the director to get with them and figure out from the very beginning, as much as he can, where he wants to go with the picture. When I find out what kind of picture they want and I tell them what kind of picture I want, we make compromises. I had no problems with *The Learning Tree*. It was my book. I wrote the screenplay. Kenny Hyman said, 'This is Gordon's film. I don't want anybody fooling with it. Let him do what he wants.' And that's the way it was, even down to the last cut.

"It was pretty much the same way with *Shaft*. Aubrey and Netter decided the type of film they wanted. They made compromises for me and I made a few for them. In the end, we came out with what we wanted: a tough, hard picture.

"Even so, I've noticed that there are some people in Hollywood who still wonder that I, a black man, can actually walk in and do this thing without having a lot of whites behind me telling me what to do. They just can't believe, when they walk into a room, that I'm going to make a decision on the type of film, the color, the choice of furniture for the room, the choice of paint for the wall, the choice of everything for that film that the director has to do."

With that attitude, would he prefer working for Hollywood or being an independent?

"Everybody would like to be independent. But there's nothing like having a big studio there to take the weight off you when you need it. I think that anyone starting out should start under the auspices of a big studio. They're going to rob you—this big overhead thing—but if you are going to learn how to make pictures well, you should have the finest facilities that you can possibly have so that you at least know what you need when you become an independent. If you don't start with everything, with the knowledge, you will miss a lot that you can't get as an independent filmmaker. Certainly, I prefer to have my own company. In a sense, M-G-M has encouraged me to have my own individual unit just to do pictures for them. Well, I'd rather have a unit just to do pictures for Gordon Parks, and I will. But I'll work with M-G-M, because I can get a lot out of any of the major studios, and I use that to gain more knowledge of what I will be doing out there as an independent."

Parks emphasized his concern about the image of blacks on the screen.

"I think that as far as blacks are concerned—not only

blacks, any group—people want to walk out of the theater after having seen themselves depicted accurately. I don't want to malign them. I don't want to try to use them, but I want to be faithful to whatever the project's purpose was. As far as blacks are concerned, they've been used so poorly in films for so many years that I instinctively try to upgrade a line or a part so as to take away the taint of the type of role the black actor used to have to play, which made me very ashamed when I was a kid. I always used to sort of hang my head. I was ashamed of what Stepin Fetchit and Louise Beavers had to do, always playing the low-down parts. Without actually declaring it, I just sort of knew that if I ever got to be a director, I would try to help get rid of this stigma. I think I have in *The Learning Tree*, and I have in *Shaft*. *Shaft* comes out a marvelous hero that both black and white kids can look up to as a great guy."

He was asked how he interpreted his role as a black filmmaker to the black community.

"I do think that the black director, especially when he's handling pictures espousing black content, has to protect and interpret the roles in a way that will no longer be offensive to blacks. The handling of the militants, for instance, would have been very bad if it had gone the way the book was written, because they were just hanging around banging garbage cans as detractors while Shaft did his thing upstairs, rescuing the girl. I protected the part of the militant. I made it generally a stronger part to make it more reasonable in a more viable situation, and generally uplifted the parts of the blacks in *Shaft*."

Shaft opened in New York in June 1971 with a premiere on Broadway, a premiere that publicists called a "first" for the new black films on the Great White Way. It was a benefit, with the proceeds going to New York police fraternal organizations for families of those killed in the line of duty.

By the fourth week, *Shaft* was on its way to being a hit. An estimated eighty percent of the audiences were blacks. A black-owned public relations agency, the UniWorld Group, was given much of the marketing credit. Long before the premieres, UniWorld's promotion director, Bill Cherry (who also became Richard Roundtree's manager), had screened the film for "every level of the black community" in several cities and advertised in virtually every black newspaper and magazine. Although his agency only introduced the film to black people, black-directed publicity was another successful breakthrough in the industry. M-G-M later retained the agency for other work.

"If it wasn't a black film," UniWorld's president, Byron Lewis, had admitted during an interview about *Shaft* with *Variety*, "it would have been an average white film." His assessment was consistent with the general evaluation of the movie.

Reviewers for the *Los Angeles Times* and the *New York Times*, however, were even less enthusiastic. Clayton Riley, the contributing black critic for the *Times*, wrote a scathing review.

Headlined "A Black Film For White Audiences?" it attacked the directing, acting, script, and technical quality, concluding that *Shaft* was "an extended lie, a distortion that simply grows larger and more unbelievable with each frame."

Riley added, "Inevitably, *Shaft* will be compared to the title character in Melvin Van Peebles's cinematic triumph,

Sweet Sweetback's Badasssss Song. That argument is already settled for me: *Sweetback* wins in a walk. Which is, whether or not you believe a painful truth *(Sweetback)* or a soothing falsehood *(Shaft)*."

Parks, who was on assignment for *Life* in Paris, dispatched a telegram to the editor of the *New York Times*. "I don't feel any compulsion as the director of *Shaft* to defend the artistic aspects of my film. As a black artist, however, I believe it is important to help sharpen our perspectives about the portrayal of black people in motion pictures and *Shaft* in particular."

He noted that predominantly black crowds had helped the movie gross $6 million in two months. Parks answered many of Riley's specific criticisms. He pointed out that most black critics had praised the film, among them Maurice Peterson (of *Essence*), who had described *Shaft* as the "first picture to show a black man who leads a life free of racial torment."

Parks concluded: "I will hold Riley in higher esteem when he gains more experience as a reviewer of all filmmakers—not as a self-appointed executioner of blacks who have survived the purgatorial haunts of Hollywood to become directors and producers. Sheathe your borrowed sword, Mr. Riley. Your brother is not the enemy."

In his *Times* review, Riley had predicted there would be sequels to *Shaft*. Only days later producer Roger Lewis announced that, because of the film's success, he had written *The Big Bamboo,* which would again star Richard Roundtree, and would be shot in Jamaica. At least four Hollywood studios besides M-G-M expressed interest when Lewis and co-producer Stirling Silliphant confirmed plans to create a black James Bond.

The Caribbean location was selected "so that while keeping the black audience in the U.S., we will also build an international audience," Lewis explained, emphasizing that he wanted to continue using black actors, crew, and director in this new project. He also expected to have a black advisor read his screenplay.

"Black audiences have a sixth sense," he said, suddenly an expert on black people. "They know when you are putting something over on them with black actors up front." He foresaw greater opportunity for blacks in film production if his *Shaft* formula continued to work.

By the end of the year, *Shaft* had indeed worked, grossing in excess of $15 million even before international distribution, and coincidentally pulling M-G-M out of fiscal difficulty.

There were difficulties in getting the second film started, however. Location was shifted to New York when problems arose in Chicago; it was the second switch since the producers had scrapped their original plan to film in Jamaica. Then Roundtree, who had starred in the first picture for $13,500, demanded a salary more in keeping with his brief but impressive track record. With the support of Parks, he won.

For the second time, Parks finished ahead of schedule. Post-production chores were also accelerated, and the sequel to *Shaft* was in theaters only thirteen months after the opening of its predecessor. It was technically a better production, and initial response was encouraging, but the film, now titled *Shaft's Big Score,* was not more effective. Not only Clayton Riley penned a poor review this time.

Nevertheless, when *Shaft's Big Score* was opening around the country, Parks went to Detroit to receive the

NAACP's Spingarn Award, his first major honor from a black organization.

By then, he was hedging about doing a third Shaft film, though seven had been planned. He mentioned alternate possibilities that included filming in Europe with stars like James Earl Jones and scripts by some of the best writers in Hollywood. "I've done two Shaft films now and I want to move on. I want to do films like *any* other director in Hollywood would do. I think I'm ready now."

9

Melvin Van Peebles

In 1967 the San Francisco Film Festival Award was presented to a foreign entry, *The Story of a Three Day Pass*. The film's director was originally from Chicago, but he came to the festival as a French delegate. He had spent ten years abroad painting and writing, and finally he directed (in Paris) his first feature film. Melvin Van Peebles surprised many of his compatriots by winning the award. He created the bittersweet story of an American soldier who spends a seventy-two-hour pass with a French girl.

After an absence of black movie directors and the misuse of black film artists for three decades, Van Peebles was a logical choice to bring relevant black themes to the screen. The award embarrassed Hollywood, but offers came from several studios that would have liked to make Van Peebles their token black American director. He turned them down.

He had worked as a gripman on a San Francisco trolley after a tour as an Air Force navigator. With a photographer friend, Ruth Bernhard, he had written *The Big*

Heart, a book about the cable car run, while learning filmmaking. After watching a movie in a San Francisco theater and seeing black life so poorly depicted that he knew he could do better, he sold his car and made three short films. In 1954, he took these films to Hollywood in search of a beginner's job in the industry. He was offered jobs as elevator operator and parking lot attendant. He went to Europe.

Only after Gordon Parks and Ossie Davis had come on the scene did Van Peebles accept a Columbia Pictures offer to direct *Watermelon Man,* a satire about an obnoxious white businessman who one day mysteriously wakes up black.

With money he earned from *Watermelon Man* (which was a moderate success) and a $50,000 loan from Bill Cosby, thirty-eight-year-old Van Peebles opted to forego his three-picture studio contract and make a "revolutionary" independent film. In less time than many features go through pre-production, he directed, produced, scored, and starred in *Sweet Sweetback's Badasssss Song* and watched as it rose, albeit controversially, to make more money than any other movie in the country for three weeks in May and two more in October.

The Cinemation release, full of coarse but realistic dialogue and imagery, told the story of the radicalization and subsequent revolt against society by a black stud. It grossed over $10 million in its first run. Filmed in southern California in twenty days by Van Peebles's one-man production company, Yeah Inc., it became one of the most lucrative independent films ever made. (The scoring, editing, and opticals took another seven months.)

Before its release, Van Peebles had said the film had

"violence, action, sex, and lots of niggers," and he described *Sweetback* as relevant.

"To make a relevant film in Hollywood is not the easiest
of tasks," he said. "The battle for the minds of black
people is a very important battle. If you're going to make
a relevant thing, you need your own communications
system. It's impossible to get financing and make a
movie the way I want to. What they consider a little control, I consider extreme control. They want a very strong
say, including the last word . . . the final cut. But that
is a right they assure you they'll never exercise. It's like a
knife hanging over your head."

Nine days before the first opening of *Sweetback*, Van
Peebles, flanked by two attorneys and an American Civil
Liberties Union official, threatened, at a press conference, to sue the Motion Picture Association of America
(MPAA) unless his film was given a "non-rating," at least
for black audiences. He accused the MPAA of participating in "cultural genocide" by imposing white judgment on
black-oriented subject matter. "I refuse to submit this
film," he said, "neither will I self-apply an X-rating to
my movie, if such a rating is to be applicable to black
audiences."

Van Peebles had already voluntarily submitted his
independent film to the MPAA and paid the fee to have
it screened. It had been X-rated, theoretically barring
audiences under age seventeen. Van Peebles protested,
and his theater billboards and New York newspaper ads
proclaimed, "Rated X by an all-white jury."

Jack Valenti, president of the MPAA, responded to the
challenge in less than a week. In a letter to Van Peebles
that was made public, Valenti wrote that "films are not

rated on the basis of race. They are rated solely on the basis of informing parents about the content of the film—all parents, black and white."

But these were the problems of the independent, non-union filmmaker, particularly when he was black.

Van Peebles owned distribution rights to the film, but he worked out a seven-year lease with the New York-based Cinemation Industries, previously known for marketing films on the exploitation circuit. Van Peebles spent his advertising dollars buying time on black radio stations. The film premiered in New York in a special midnight screening at the 125th Street Loew's in Harlem; a similar opening was held in Watts, California.

Only two theaters in the country would book it. The Detroit Grand Circus had been averaging $4,000 a week playing third- and fourth-run pictures. *Sweetback* opened there on March 30, grossing over $200,000 in its first four weeks. The Coronet Theater in Atlanta agreed to show the film, and it smashed existing house records there as it had in Detroit.

When *Sweetback* got to Boston, theater owner Ben Sack had nine minutes deleted from the film, and Van Peebles filed and won a suit in federal court to have the material restored to the film.

He was asked what he planned to do concerning his threatened action against the MPAA.

"I'm suing them. I'm fighting them. That's all I can do. It's a long-drawn-out process; it's a lot of bread. Everybody's mumbling, talking about this isn't revolutionary, brother, that isn't revolutionary, but nobody has come forward to help me find the bread, pay the lawyers."

Van Peebles was soon as controversial as his film. He

appeared on "The David Frost Show," but at the height
of *Sweetback's* box office success, he was ignored by the
three network late-night talk shows. His movie was reviewed by *Variety, Cue, New York,* and *Newsweek,* but
it was ignored by *Time, Life, Look,* and the *New York
Daily News.* Because it was a major movie, making major
money, Van Peebles was not happy at being snubbed, and
he revealed his dissatisfaction in a *Variety* interview.

He was asked how much the white audience is a consideration to the black director.

"It's a consideration. It depends where your head is at.
If you're making a film that costs $20 million, then you
have to think not only in terms of the white audience but
of the worldwide audience to hope to get back your nut.
It depends, however; if you can forego the feeling of
being loved by all and forego the budget the devil requires
and also the insipidness the devil requires, you can go for
broke."

The *New York Times* did respond to *Sweetback.* In the
Sunday Arts and Leisure section, Vincent Canby wrote an
extensive, searching review. Equal space was afforded
Clayton Riley in the same issue. Riley, whose enthusiasm
for the film was challenged in Harlem at a weekend panel
discussion, wrote a column interpreting the film in the
New York Amsterdam News. Weeks later, he wrote a
review of Gordon Parks's *Shaft* and said that in comparison, *Sweetback* was far more significant as a black man's
movie.

Sweetback was described as "a truly black film," and
Van Peebles, at least, considered his movie revolutionary.
One of the most gratifying affirmations of that appraisal
must have been when a national black newspaper devoted

a twelve-page supplement to a detailed analysis of the film. *Sweetback* had become number one on the chart a month earlier, so the effect of Defense Minister Huey Newton's scene-by-scene review (in the Black Panther newspaper on June 19) was uncertain. An accolade that even included four Biblical quotations, it was a fascinating argument for black community support of the film.

"On many levels," Newton wrote, "Van Peebles is attempting to communicate some crucial ideas and motivate us to a deeper understanding and then action based on that understanding. He has certainly made effective use of one of the most popular forms of communication—the movie—and he is dealing in revolutionary terms."

Newton believed many who had seen the film had missed its significance. He had seen it several times and had understood more each time.

"When Bobby and I started the Black Panther Party, we wanted to build in the black community the love, the sacredness, and the unity we so desperately need," he said. "This is still our goal, and we try by administering our many survival programs. *Sweet Sweetback* helps to put forth the ideas of what we must do to build that community. We need to see it often and learn from it."

An equally extensive (7½ pages) analysis of Van Peebles's film and philosophy appeared in the September issue of *Ebony*, about the time *Sweetback's* second run began in some two hundred theaters across the country. Senior editor Lerone Bennett's byline appeared above the article "The Emancipation Orgasm: Sweetback in Wonderland."

The *Sweetback* phenomenon was growing. Sweatshirts and other trivia circulated. *Newsweek, Show,* and finally

Time and *Life* had done features on Van Peebles, though
they had avoided reviewing the movie. In August, and
again in September, the director appeared on "The Dick
Cavett Show." And with the *Ebony* article, which was
recognition by the most widely-read black periodical and
its most prominent writer, few areas of the public domain
were left untouched.

Bennett wrote that "*Sweet Sweetback,* despite its acclaim and despite isolated moments of promise, is a trivial
and tasteless negative classic: trivial and tasteless because
of the banality of conception and execution; a negative
classic, because it is an obligatory step for anyone who
wants to go further and make the first black revolutionary
film. This is a judgment that one wishes that he did not
have to make, but it is a judgment that one must make,
not only because *Sweet Sweetback's* success seems likely
to lead to a number of imitative Sons of Sweetback, but
also because many blacks are suffering under the illusion
that the film is revolutionary and black.

"*Sweet Sweetback* is neither revolutionary nor black,"
he continued. "Instead of giving us new images of black
rebels, it carries us back to antiquated white stereotypes,
subtly and invidiously identified with black reality. Instead of carrying us forward to the new frontier of col-
lective action, it drags us back to the pre-Watts days of
isolated individual acts of resistance, conceived in confusion and executed in panic."

After a discussion of the sex and the black images in
the film, Bennett concluded: "Mr. Van Peebles is a winner
now. Like Sweetback, he has proven that you can mess
with The Man and escape, if not win. But his escape, like
Sweetback's, is tinged with a thousand ironies; for, in the

Butterfly McQueen in *Mildred Pierce*. (Warner Bros.)

Sidney Poitier starring in and directing *A Warm December*. (National General)

Bill Cosby with his old sidekick, Robert Culp, in *Hickey and Boggs*. (United Artists)

Billie Dee Williams as Billie Holiday's husband in *Lady Sings the Blues*. (Paramount)

Director Gordon Parks, the first black man to direct a major film (M-G-M)

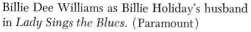

Soul singer Wilson Pickett in *Soul to Soul*. (Cinerama Releasing)

Willie Best and Bob Hope in *The Ghost Breakers*. (Paramount)

James Edwards and Lloyd Bridges in *Home of the Brave*. (Stanley Kramer)

Lucia Moses in *Scar of Shame*.

John Killens, screenwriter,
Odds Against Tomorrow.

Paul Robeson.

Dooley Wilson, Humphrey Bogart, Ingrid Bergman in *Casablanca*. (Warner Bros.)

John Hodiak, Canada Lee, Tallulah Bankhead in *Lifeboat*. (20th Century)

Shirley Temple and Bill "Bojangles" Robinson in *The Little Colonel*. (Fox)

James Earl Jones portrayed fighter Jack Johnson in both stage and film versions of *The Great White Hope*. (20th Century-Fox)

Shaft's Big Score, starring Richard Roundtree. (M-G-M)

final analysis, he won or escaped not on his own terms, but on The Man's terms and in terms of The Man's myths and philosophy (entertainment vs. instruction) and brilliant marketing techniques."

In Van Peebles's home town of Chicago, the Kuumba Workshop, a group of seventy actors, writers, painters, singers, dancers, and others, aged six to sixty, with creative interests, embarked on a national campaign of "black awakening and assertion" to alert black people to what they believed to be dangers and distortions in the film. There was a public forum on July 23 at the Holy Angels Church, where a Kuumba position paper was distributed to artists, ministers, activists, and organizational leaders, as well as to the mass media. A concerted effort to locate other groups throughout the country who shared their views and would take similar steps to organize opposition in their localities was also announced.

Kuumba's director, Mrs. Val Gray Ward, called *Sweet-back* "nothing more than a hustle of black people's money, fears, weaknesses, desire to see themselves in movies, and the sexual hangups of a relatively few blacks. That's why we're appalled by the filth, degradation, distortion, and almost total negativism of *Sweetback*—both as a movie and as a social statement to black people."

Van Peebles was contemptuous of blacks who didn't accept his film. He was asked if black people had difficulty grasping messages in films.

"I think that any American's mind has a degree of colonization," he said. "I don't know about others, but this particular film is a complete breakaway from a certain way of thinking which leads intellectually into more difficulty for understanding. The intellectual has been trained

to lean against something or into something. He has no
material in his computer for understanding what he sees
[in *Sweetback*]. He needs a whole new program. This can
be very confusing and it leads to a great deal of misunderstanding."

On the evening of Sunday, September 12, Van Peebles
appeared on the first annual "Sickle Cell Anemia Tele-
thon," at Lincoln Center. He previewed a segment of his
forthcoming Broadway production, *Ain' Supposed to Die
a Natural Death,* and made an appeal for funds. He spoke
briefly on the controversy about his film, conceding that
many did not like *Sweetback,* but defending his role
and contributions as an independent director who had
beaten the system.

Things were anything but bad. When *Variety* hit the
stands three days later, not only was *Sweetback* ahead of
other productions, *Black Jesus, Soul to Soul,* and *Shaft,* but
also, after only two weeks of its second run, it was again
the top box office movie in the country. Having grossed
$387,000 by the end of the week of September 8, it sus-
tained its position for a second such week.

Van Peebles stayed in the limelight on television talk
shows, and when he was introduced by a "Today Show"
interviewer as "the most successful black producer," he
immediately corrected her; the box office results had made
him "*the* most successful producer."

Would *Sweetback* set a trend in black filmmaking?
"Well, the film made money," Van Peebles replied. "It's
traditional that a cycle will start showing itself. It
wouldn't surprise me if we had a number of imitators."

Van Peebles was asked to define the impact of *Sweetback.*

"I think it's decolonizing minds," he said. "It also shows, as a side product, that blacks—because ninety-five percent of the people at this stage of the game who have seen it are blacks—have made it number one, which means we have a viable industry of our own."

On the eve of the opening of his play, Van Peebles appeared on NET's "Black Journal," in a segment called "Is Sweetback Really Sweet?" Also on the program, with interviewer Tony Brown, was Van Peebles's ally Clayton Riley, along with Francis Ward of Kuumba, and Peter Bailey of *Ebony*. The remarks of Ward and Bailey were acerbic. The interviews had been filmed separately, however, and there was no forum where the protagonists could confront one another. This option was offered when another NET program, "Free Time," announced it would produce a ninety-minute program on black films.

In October, when the National Association of Theater Owners met in New York, Cinemation president Jerry Gross said he might undertake a film adaptation of *Ain' Supposed to Die a Natural Death,* which Van Peebles predicted would run on Broadway for three years.

With his Boston lawsuit in mind, Van Peebles addressed the theater owners, advising them that he "didn't want any static" with any future projects. Static had appeared earlier that fall, when the government of Australia refused to accept *Sweetback,* reportedly because of "violence" in the film. Closer to home, Miami theater owners refused to book the film after Florida's Assistant State Attorney, Leonard Rivkind, threatened legal proceedings if the film was shown.

On the West Coast, the Hollywood chapter of the

NAACP voted Van Peebles the Best Director Award for *Sweetback* at their annual Image Awards dinner.

In New Mexico a few months later, Van Peebles filmed his fourth feature, *Don't Play Us Cheap*, which opened as his second Broadway play soon afterward.

Even with two plays on Broadway, new record albums, and continued writing, Van Peebles had left his most important mark on America—and its film industry—with *Sweet Sweetback's Badasssss Song*.

As controversy about him and his movie continued, Van Peebles was asked where he would go next.

"I'll do whatever comes to me naturally," he replied. "I won't be blackmailed by my failures, and I won't be blackmailed by my successes either. I'll do what I feel like doing when I feel like doing it."

One can argue about *Sweetback* almost endlessly. Are its images positive or negative? Are they negative only because of what blacks think whites will read into them? Finally, does *Sweetback* work as propaganda to further the cause of black people? However one answers these questions, one fact is established: *Sweetback's* political importance outweighs its artistry; Van Peebles's achievement is noteworthy even more for its initiative than for its merit. If there had been a hundred films controlled and directed by blacks, *Sweetback* (or its equivalent) would have been made years ago and would have had only historical, if any, significance at this time.

10

Ossie Davis: First Harlem, Then the Third World

One reason there had been so few black films was their obvious commercial risk. Since Hollywood had been tightening its belt by decreasing its production, black films were automatic budgetary victims, even those with the high artistic standard of *Nothing but a Man.*

This trend was challenged in 1969, when Ossie Davis, a black theater director and well-known stage and screen actor, directed *Cotton Comes to Harlem,* a film based on Chester Himes's 1964 comic-dramatic novel. It had an impressive cast of popular black stars—Godfrey Cambridge, Raymond St. Jacques, Calvin Lockhart, Cleavon Little, and Judy Pace—and a number of blacks in the production crew.

Filmed almost entirely in Harlem, the off-beat detective story had moments of homespun satire despite many Hollywood gags and gimmicks. Box office reaction was enthusiastic, and besides being popular with black audiences, *Cotton* also attracted white moviegoers.

There was talk of a sequel and perhaps a series on the order of the James Bond thrillers. But it was close to six months before the film broke even, and producer Sam Goldwyn, Jr. found United Artists unwilling to finance a sequel. The film eventually grossed over $6 million, but by then the cast had moved on to other projects.

Davis had gone to Nigeria to direct his second film, *Kongi's Harvest,* a satire on contemporary African politics with a screenplay by Nigerian writer Wole Soyinka. Filmed for Calpenny Ltd., with an all-African cast, it was the first major motion picture produced in English by an African movie company.

Davis returned to New York with his film, and when production chores were completed, he found that the major distributors were unwilling to handle it. Paramount, Warners, United Artists, Columbia, and others turned down the film as "too special, too African" for mass distribution.

Davis described the film as "a comedy of African politics." "It is unusual," he said, "a first of its kind, as it shows Africa as Africans see it. No attempt was made to change it or adjust it for the peculiarities of any particular filmgoers, American or otherwise."

In April 1971 the film premiered in Lagos, Nigeria and was greeted by standing ovations, Davis reported. But back in New York, screenings failed to attract potential distributors even after the film had been recut.

Davis did not agree with the reasons for the refusals. He suggested to *Variety,* "Maybe they are frightened. Africa without Tarzan may be too raw, too threatening, too strong for their blood, but that's exactly why we made *Kongi's Harvest.* I am prejudiced, for after all, I did direct the film. And while I myself am not an African, I am an Afro-American. There's not that much difference."

He described events that led to production of the film.

"In 1967, Wole Soyinka came to America. He had formed Calpenny-Nigeria, Ltd., a film company. 'Cal' stood for California, 'pen' stood for Pennsylvania, and 'ny' for New York. They wanted to form a company with both U.S. and African components. They were able to raise $10,000 from African students here. They were becoming involved in executing film projects, and they wanted my assistance. I had spent thirty-two months in Africa in World War II, in Liberia, Nigeria, Ghana, Egypt, and the Sudan. So Africa was not foreign to me. Now, there will always be in America more black people with talent than jobs. It was true then, it's true now, and it will be true for a damn long time to come. There were just so many of us who had no chance to be employed in this racist society. That was some situation. We had the skills and they had the need. There were fruitful possibilities. If we were going to go to the mother country, I thought we should take something with us. After all, black people were mutually affected by western suppression: racism on this side, colonialism on the other."

Continuing, he said, "I indicated that I would act, if necessary, and direct, if wanted. In 1967, a civil war broke out and everything was held in abeyance.

"Finally, an arrangement was worked out where Calpenny would work with Herald Productions, which had done *Putney Swope*, and Omega Productions, a Swedish group, whereby all would share one-third of the profit. Omega went to Africa and drew up a budget and also provided our crew. We made the film in six weeks, but it was by no means an ideal situation. It was only one month after the war, and there were many problems. Some we were able to solve, some we were not."

On the problem of distribution, he recommended an alternative. "I think we should work toward setting up a chain of theaters in black communities in the United States, in the West Indies and in the English-speaking countries of Africa. The most active film audience is the black audience—if we had a way to get to our own people of Africa and South America. We are after more than having a film and having somebody else show it for us, which is the way it is now. We have to think organization. We have to become entrepreneurs. Black people are already out there waiting with the money in their hands. And some black people already own theaters."

As for the feasibility of such an arrangement, he commented, "Blacks are to be included if there's gonna be any film industry at all. I'm sure of that. The day will come when the black community has set up a chain of theaters around the world, when we are not dependent on The Man for anything."

Why hadn't black businessmen supported established black filmmakers?

"Films are risky. We can't afford to risk it in the beginning. If we use outside financing, we will prove that it can be done while we are also giving ourselves skills. When we have this, then we have stability. Right now, we lack organization because it is to somebody's great profit that we do.

"The black community spends between $30 and $40 billion a year," he pointed out. "But the day will come when black companies will support black filmmakers. The time is not just yet. We can't attack frontally. We have to be careful. There are too many wolves out there. We can't desire to do it and think that is enough."

What ideas and innovations will be displayed in black theaters of the future?

"I haven't the slightest idea, but I know it's going to be fantastic. It's going to lift the eyelids off the whole world. The trumpet was a western instrument but the black man learned to play it and he created jazz. That was something that had never been heard before. I'll be looking to the black filmmakers of the future and saying, 'Bring me some jazz in that film.' We can't be playing with it. That's what The Man did. He didn't need it for anything. There is a revolutionary thing that needs to be done. Film will help us do it. We have to do it with communications. We have to find ways to tell our people what we are and what we are going to do. We were always a vocal people, not readers. We've got to say what we want to be on the face of the earth. Film is going to be one of the most effective ways of saying what we want to say. In *Kongi* we were not able to do justice to what Africa is all about. In the future we must find a film that can relate to us all.

"We need films with interest and we need cultural entertainment. Equally important is what we are trying to say, what we want our people to see. We must get our own black images. And if we can communicate human feeling, then we are doing something important."

What should the black director try to accomplish?

"The black filmmaker should try to express in film the truth of the black experience as it happened and is happening on this side of the ocean, on the Caribbean islands, in South America and in Africa. I think there is a common

element in the black man's history due to slavery and due
to dispersal of blacks from the African continent all over
the world, but I think that common tie is still a part of
what we are, and I think the black filmmakers all over
should begin to find out those things which reunite us and
establish us as a people. It doesn't have to be related specifically back to Africa, but to everything that is authen-
tically black, that we created, that is meaningful to us, that
we are proud of, that is as distinctively us as is jazz or the
spirituals or soul. Translating these elements to film, that's
what the black filmmaker should be doing."

Subjectively, he added: "If I can be instrumental in
helping bring from the Hollywood machinery the techniques, the skills, then I feel I am accomplishing something. I have to make deals, but I justify it by being a
bridge and opening doors for training of young blacks."

Asked if he planned a "personal statement" film like
Gordon Parks's *The Learning Tree* or Melvin Van
Peebles's *Sweetback*, he said no. "What I want to do is a
film which will star my wife, and I just finished writing
the script. I've been working on it for five years and it's a
film, but it's not a personal statement. It's a film that in-
vestigates the relationship between the United States'
corporate structure and the African countries which produce the raw materials these corporate people use. What
happens when an African country wants to free itself
from a white corporation and the black people involved
in the corporation? How are black people used in relation to African people?"

Fifteen months after Davis had begun distributors'
screenings of *Kongi's Harvest*, a new company called TAM
Communications acquired distribution rights to the film

and scheduled a June opening in Washington, D. C. TAM, a team of three black businessmen (Charles Grigsby, B. M. Lee, and R. A. League), announced plans to distribute "genuine films about black people" as opposed to "the current wave of so-called black films [which] simply exploit the black moviegoing public by offering black faces in white roles and pretending to offer reality."

Davis sidestepped the planned sequel to *Cotton*, keeping active in community and national causes, including the fund-raising for Angela Davis. Rumors of his disagreement with producer Goldwyn over the handling of black experience in future films were ultimately confirmed by Davis, who also had misgivings about his own involvement with *Cotton*.

By midsummer he was back in Hollywood directing the screen version of the off-Broadway success, *Black Girl*, with Leslie Uggams in the leading role.

Davis considers himself primarily a writer, and he is uncomfortable working in a Hollywood setting. In whatever he does, his primary goal is artistic independence.

"There are a lot of young black independent filmmakers today who are on their own and doing films without any restrictions, doing things the way they see them. I think that day will come for all of us in the industry."

11

William Greaves:
Doing His Own Thing

A lot of people make movies—on campuses, in the ghetto, in skyscrapers, in shuttered motel rooms, and on military reservations. For training, for fun, for a hobby, or for profit, amateur and professional motion picture lovers do their own thing.

Opportunities for independent filmmakers are increasing, and many blacks have chosen this route to circumvent the Hollywood establishment. When the West Coast film center was struggling to make a comeback, New York entered into the competition. Results indicate it may become *the* center for black filmmaking. One man who would certainly deserve much of the credit is a prolific filmmaker who grew up in Harlem and acted in the theater and motion pictures with moderate success. As a young man he competed with Poitier and Belafonte for stage parts before becoming interested in film production. His name is William Greaves.

"It was pretty clear to me back in 1952," he explained in *Jet* Magazine, "when I was trying to crack into the industry, that there was a wall of racism and discrimination that I could not possibly penetrate."

Like Melvin Van Peebles, he was forced to go abroad. For more than ten years he worked for Canada's National Film Board as writer, chief editor, assistant director, or director on nearly eighty films.

Returning to the United States in 1963, he became a producer for United Nations television, producing three films before starting his own company. William Greaves Productions leased its president to National Educational Television in New York, where for a few months he was executive producer of "Black Journal," the Emmy-Award-winning, black-oriented network news show. But he soon returned to New York and began seeking contracts to produce independent films. In 1970, he won ten major awards for film and television productions about the black man's problems, ambitions, and future in America.

But Greaves was also in sympathy with the struggle of other minorities. *Voice of La Raza,* his film about the prejudice and job discrimination affecting ten million Spanish-speaking Americans, starred the Mexican-born actor Anthony Quinn. The documentary, sponsored by the Equal Employment Opportunity Commission, won another film award for William Greaves.

Two superstars in a different profession were the subject of a 1971 Greaves production. Most heavyweight title fights through the years have been known as "the fight of the century," but when Muhammed Ali, a poet, and Joe Frazier, a nightclub singer, met in Madison Square Garden, they were promised $2.5 million apiece to go fifteen rounds. The money alone made the fight something special. No television rights were sold, so there were large audiences when Greaves's filmed highlights were shown in theaters across the nation. Later in the year he began a feature film about the fight.

Like Gordon Parks, Greaves has a son starting in the film business as well as a brother. His son was editing film in another room when Greaves was interviewed at his West 54th Street office one afternoon.

Greaves discussed black films. "There are probably three different areas. One is the Hollywood area. It fulfills the Hollywood establishment's commercial requirements. Then you've got what you would call the public service type of film—the documentary, ranging from the public affairs films on television to sponsored films for various institutions—some of them educational, some with social welfare objectives, some for the government. The last is clearly the independent cat who is out there. He's got himself four, five thousand dollars as a grant to make a film, or he's begged, borrowed, and stolen enough money from relatives to go out and do his thing."

Who *is* the independent?

"He's more often the product of a film workshop or a film school or some black community center that's got this equipment lying there to be used. I think this is the most honest, the most unfettered. It's here that you get the freest kind of expression. But herein also lies a problem. The overwhelming majority of people working in that area are not really experienced, so those films are almost always deficient technically or artistically in one way or another, but they are still the most candid in a way."

About public affairs, he said, "I think it's in the public affairs sector that you get both the professional and the candid expression. They call it 'black consciousness.' You have a certain amount of institutional influence on the films, but they are of a much better order than, let's say, Hollywood. There's much less uptightness about certain kinds of issues being aired. Of course, it changes when you are doing public affairs for a commercial network or for educational television. Educational television will give you a more candid film. I think the best illustration of that is the work we did with 'Black Journal' and the work that continues there."

Can an honest film—an honest black film—be made in Hollywood?

"Yes and no. The major part of the answer is no—absolutely not. That has to be qualified, because Hollywood is a strange animal. That is to say, if it comes to pass that the filmmaker is talented or sensational, then he is accorded a range of freedoms and license which the other guy, though successful, will not be given. For example, Melvin Van Peebles does *Sweet Sweetback's Badasssss Song*. Now I've never seen the film, but I'm told it's very unorthodox. He could have been seriously stopped as a result but as it turns out, for some strange sort of chemical reason it caught on like wildfire, and maybe it's because it's a very good film.

"Whatever the reason, Melvin is now moving very rapidly. Now in these circumstances, it's easier for him to get money to do another film which is bizarre and unorthodox. It's the bizarre and unorthodox that has made him successful, and Wall Street investors are people who are interested in making money, so they would put up their money for the bizarre and unorthodox from Melvin Van Peebles, but not from anybody else. The next fact is that the white American, and more specifically the racist American mind, sees anything that relates to black manhood or freedom of expression for the black community as bizarre and unorthodox. Therefore, it's conceivable that Van Peebles will emerge as a very free agent in Hollywood. Having said that, he would be, more or less, the exception to the rule."

Would the situation improve? "I think that it will become increasingly possible—and I may be foolishly optimistic—that because of the commercial factor and candor that are becoming increasingly popular, black filmmakers, who are more candid and speak from areas that the wider community has little contact with, will probably flourish in this country.

"Personally, I have earned something of a reputation of being reasonably independent. It is because of this independence that I have been successful, and when I am approached to do films, there is not too much of a tendency to constrain or restrain me. They feel my films will be good, because the impact of my films often trades on their being innovative and independent in thinking. Again, 'Black Journal,' under my executive producership, was considered very militant and a radical kind of show. Everyone thought we were going to be thrown off the air. It came to pass that the shows were of sufficient quality and spoke of information that not only the black community wanted to hear but the white community, even the reactionaries, were utterly fascinated with. Their morbid anxieties and fears were of such a nature that they really dreaded talking to blacks on a one-to-one basis about how they really felt, but if they could, under a cold television, tune in and find out what those darkies were thinking, that was fascinating to them. It became so fascinating we won the Emmy."

Asked if he felt black filmmakers had been successful in communicating, he said, "As far as I'm concerned, all the films we've done, for 'Black Journal' or otherwise, have been successful, and I don't think we've had any difficulty in communicating our intentions to either the black community or the white community. I think it should be pointed out that I have been making films for twenty-one years. Filmmaking is like medicine, architecture, like any sophisticated professional enterprise. The individual has to go through a number of developmental stages. You're in a communications medium where you are trying to communicate ideas. The efficiency and the clarity with which you communicate your ideas is a function, not only of the content of your ideas, but your operational experience with the medium. So that you would use the language of film, the grammar of film, the syntax of film, the whole vocabulary of film, to make a proper translation into cinematic language of what is inside your head."

How important is the white audience to the black filmmaker?

"Let me say that I came into motion pictures because I was very uptight, very angry with the way black people— the black experience—was depicted, if it was depicted at all. I would say that the bulk of my films are geared to dealing with the black experience in one way or another, or those events which touch upon the black experience.

"Having said that, I'm certainly interested in creative and artistic issues too, because I am also an artist. I'm also a businessman in that I have to make sure we have a financial base to operate on. Since I realize that I may subvert my intention of doing films for blacks by not having a good enough base to proceed on, I'm not that much of a prisoner to black films, although it is my center of gravity."

Greaves said distribution remained a large obstacle, but that improvement had begun.

"There are a number of rumblings from various people in that direction. We are involved here in the distribution of some of our films. We have a director of distribution and we're expanding our distribution department. It's true that there is a black consumership in the various urban areas throughout the country, and there are something like twelve or thirteen hundred black-surrounded theaters which would form the basis of a black distribution circuit. Once that particular network has been linked up in a systematic way—so that an organization can effectively tap it at will—it becomes a resource of financing for black films. That means, obviously, if a black producer knows he can recover $200,000 from that circuit in terms of profit, he can then go out and make a film that is totally black for $200,000. He can't go above that, however. He can then go and earn even more dollars from the white community. At least he knows he has a guaranteed income."

As to the problems of such a circuit, he said, "The complication there is that the exhibitors in this black-surrounded circuit are, I would say, ninety-nine percent white.

"The next question is: Will a white exhibitor in a racist society take a product which is antithetical to his personal interest, his personal feeling? In other words, will this feeling cause him to resist this black-conceived product? That is a very interesting problem, and I think if he begins to see how much money is being made from it, he will yield to that, because he's basically a business-man. On the other side of the coin, he will make no effort—either because of racism or indifference, which is an aspect of racism—to seek out this kind of black prod-uct and would probably more often than not be resistant to it.

"I've gone to the Apollo Theater, which is a classic example of what I'm talking about, and seen the most vacuous, insipid, stupid, arrogant piece of white cine-matic racism that you would ever find anywhere in the world. There were all these black people with afros and dashikis; into their black bag. Waiting for Roberta Flack, they were sitting looking at this travesty. The nerve, the temerity, the gall of management to put on something of this nature! On the other side of the coin, I have given the Apollo a film that we did that was aimed at both the white and black communities. It was about black, so-called hard core, unemployed. This film did play at the Apollo, and my understanding was that it was a con-siderable success. The responses were marvelous. But I made the effort. The Apollo did not make the effort of seeking black films. If they were really hip, what they would do, now that there is this increasing body of films made by black producers, would be to find a means of seeking them out to try and make the Apollo—which is a logical place for it—the premiering center for black films." In 1973 the Apollo management did make an effort to book several Hollywood black-oriented premieres into the theater. When their efforts initially failed, they took their case to the community and the black media and ultimately won.

Greaves foresees greater development. "I certainly think there is a future for black films, a bright one. I think it will be something like the same thing that has happened with black music. Our music, our speech, our behavior, and general life styles have been unique, but accepted and absorbed into society. Just like there is a steady growth and acceptance of new black publications, I feel the same will happen with black films. I think the initial reaction to the black films that have been released in the past few years is suggestive of a trend that is just beginning to show itself."

12

St. Clair Bourne: Power to the Future

An effective answer to a persistent critic is: If you don't like the way I do my thing, why don't you do it better?

Without antagonism, anger, or invective, veteran film-makers are challenging young Black America to make films they admit could never have been made by their generation. Some past masters have philosophies, ideals, and goals that do not always coincide with those of men barely old enough to date their daughters. Directors like Parks, Van Peebles, Davis, and Greaves will continue to work, but if there is to be a distinctive black film, it must logically come from younger men.

And many are waiting for the chance. There are two groups: the independent free-lance producers, and producers who work for black film companies.

New York has long been an entertainment and communications center. When Hollywood was in its heyday, the big studios had New York offices that watched for new talent on Broadway; some of them still do. The nation's largest black population is also in New York, where Har-

lem is the training ground for many black musicians and
actors. Numerous black filmmakers believe New York
is the place for them to start, and later, to be from.

St. Clair Bourne is one of the new black filmmakers.
After learning the fundamentals under Bill Greaves at
"Black Journal," he organized his own production company, Chamba, which in Swahili means "images of the
eye."

While still developing, twenty-eight-year-old Bourne
and his associates were making films chiefly for outside
groups, building a national reputation in the process. They
were not establishment men, and only their lack of funds
prevented them from pursuing personal goals.

Bourne was one of five in the original company who
were tuned in to the new black dialogue. Through feed-
back from college campuses where he taught and lectured,
and through seeking out blacks on a trip to Europe,
Bourne has prepared to meet the challenge.

Fresh from a fact-finding tour in London and Paris,
Bourne talked about black films. "I think there are two
types of black films. One is the integrated Hollywood film
and the other is the authentic black film made by blacks
themselves.

"I see that, overall, Hollywood pulled out the black
theme as a titillation for the white audience. You know,
Putney Swope, which really wasn't Hollywood, but still
that kind of thing. It was a real potent thrust in terms of
power, but it seems to me that it was a money-making
thing rather than an overt move.

"Here was something that people would look at on television—anything black—so you put it on the screen, and

the black revolution became a pretty salable commodity. And then, there were the sort of jokes like *Watermelon Man*. I kind of think what's happening now, frankly, is that white people are tired of that, and they'll retire it for a while. All of this, incidentally, did give some [black] folks some jobs and a chance to get some skills."

What about the black characters in later Hollywood films?

"I would say that generally all the roles played served a purpose in some way. The key was to keep the white audiences entertained. Now, 'entertained' can be thrilling, it can be scary, it can make them laugh. Very rarely does a realistic role make anybody want to come back and pay more money. I guess I have to echo the charge that most of the roles were unrealistic—no, that they were shallow. They ranged from shallowness to outright false creation. And it was all for one purpose: to get the audience titillated but not really personally involved, just enough to come out and spend that three dollars. From musicals to the black revolution theme, that's basically where your two extremes are."

How would Bourne deal with a feature film he directed?

"I've changed. I kind of figure that I'm going to try to get away from really stagy situations and figures. I'm really very much on two levels. I'm on a self-examination thing. To me, the film thing is kind of an art, and I'm going to examine a lot of my experiences as a black person through art. I've been working on one script for a year and a half. It's basically the story of a guy who grew up in the middle class, who at roughly twenty-five years discovers that his parents were wrong. They didn't lie to him, but they were wrong. I'm going to deal with that. I'm going to try to deal with black man-woman relationships—love. You know, real love, not the cat's a pimp, his woman's a prostitute, and how they make it hustling The Man. No, an honest relationship. The other thing is feature films. I want to do feature films, but not in the strict Hollywood sense."

What insights had his trip to Europe provided?

"My trip to Europe showed me that you can make a good, competent narrative story without getting into that whole Hollywood thing. You can have small crews. You can shoot in a natural setting as opposed to building a set. That's what I'm going to try to do. It was very encouraging. Most of the things that my characters would revolve around, the environment that they would be in, there are places like that. Why should I have to build a Small's Paradise when, if I get the permission of the owner, I can shoot in Small's Paradise or someone's house? In any place. For example, this thing I'm working on, there's a black bourgeoisie area in Long Island called Sag Harbor. I have friends who have houses there, so why should I go out and build? I can just use a cat's house. Just from an artistic point of view, the element that I'm trying to get, I won't have to create, because it will be there. I'm going to try to get into a combination of personal statement kinds of films and examinations of people on a human, personal level rather than epic figures. Sergei Eisenstein, the Russian filmmaker, was into huge epics. His characters only played a part in terms of all the large themes like revolution and social change. My thing would be the opposite. The development of a person."

How does the subject of financing affect the young black filmmaker?

"The problem today is still that most of our funds come from white sources. We might get it through a black man in a white firm, as happened with a film financed by General Electric, but the money is still white. I think black companies like Johnson Publications would be favorable to such investments. Johnson Cosmetics has sponsored several hour-long shows for television. Of course, these shows were on black themes and were black-produced. Secondly, I think African countries would be interested and willing to finance films about themselves. Third, I think community organizations are a possible source of funding, although it might be difficult.

"At Chamba, we've gotten together a bunch of old films that were made from 1917 on, and we give three-day film festivals. That introduces the idea of black films to black people and creates a distribution system that our films can travel on, or that at least will be regularly in demand. And again, on my trip to Europe I was encouraged because there is a large West Indian community, and at least ten to fifteen organizations are there that would like to see films. The real problem is, even though it's a good point to be loose and not easily identifiable, because this protects from white exploitation, that same intangibility makes it difficult for us to create a smooth, tightly controlled distribution system. That's what we're working on now. All we have to figure out is how to officially and tightly give it to our people on a low-cost basis."

By 1973 Bourne had completed a feature-length documentary called *Let the Church Say Amen.* That fall he reconsidered his prior misgivings and accepted a grant from the American Film Institute. While in Hollywood's back yard, he kept an eye open for feature opportunities. Still, it was obvious that he was keeping his options open.

"I'd still like to make documentaries and educational films, because I think there's a need for that. Since these films are the easiest to do, they might be a good training ground for any young directors we could bring in. I'd like to have a training and informational film contract with African nations. We could use it as a basis for the transmission of not just films but a lot of other things. I'd like to be in on the development and sometimes direction, maybe just produce what people call feature films; you know, dramatic narratives for distribution commercially and on the college circuit. I'd like to be the filmmaker type. And I'd like to be the coordinator and make sure the other three levels are still going on. Plus, I'd like to teach a little bit. I think you get rejuvenated, and you have to give some of what you learn to other folks."

How will he deal with distribution of his films?

"If we do a film that is really good in professional terms and is interesting, we'll have to consider two levels of distribution. There's the mainstream market—theaters—and there's the college market, both black and white colleges. I think the college market is very lucrative these days. And it's getting better; the visual generation and all that sort of stuff. There's also an unknown and probably not analyzed market—black community organizations, professors of black studies, activist groups. There are a lot of these groups that are not identifiable by any kind of usual market analysis means, but they are there. It's just like the so-called black buying power that's now being 'discovered' but was there all along. The key is to make the cost low enough.

"I think you have to consider the whole world as a market. I mean black people besides here in America. I think we can make it if we prove we are honest and competent."

13

The Now and Future
of Black Cinema

It was 1971, and Hollywood was hurting. In the era of the forty-cent hot dog, there were all kinds of problems. In 1969, for instance, five of the seven big companies lost millions of dollars. Movies for television, high interest rates, independent production companies with winning formulas, and persistent foreign competition were discussed by worried industry executives even on psychiatrists' couches.

Charlton Heston, president of the Screen Actors Guild, told members at the annual meeting that motion picture production around the world had fallen lower than at any time in his memory.

He said difficulties had made the Hollywood studios and "feature production as we once knew it" a barren area. And yet, incredibly, "exhibitors at the same time are urgently calling for new products, but no one is rushing to make them."

By late summer, six-month statistics showed a continuing decline in employment despite efforts to improve the situation. On August 27 the governor of California, Ronald Reagan, a former actor and president of SAG and still seen in an occasional "Late Show" western, wrote a letter to President Nixon appealing for Nixon's endorsement of tax legislation to aid the industry. Around the same time, Los Angeles City Councilman Joel Wachs proposed a municipal film production bureau, using emergency federal funds to alleviate the studio employment crisis.

In September the Internal Revenue Service finally approved the Schreiber Plan, by which film production companies could accelerate feature and telefilm amortization for federal tax purposes. The development was expected to increase cash flow and reduce corporate interest costs on unamortized film inventory. It helped, but it was only a start.

Independent producers searching for other sources of financing found several major corporations (even some known to be conservative investors) willing to take chances on movies. Businesses like General Electric, Xerox, Mattel, Bristol-Myers, American Express, and Boise-Cascade, publications such as *Playboy* and *Reader's Digest*, and an advertising agency—Wells, Rich, and Greene—were interested. Corporations anticipated large profits from enterprises utilizing leisure time. Economists were predicting that Americans would eventually work a four-day week. That would mean an extra weekend night to spend at the movies, and according to industry estimates, seventy percent of movie attendance was on weekends.

Corporate investors at first stuck cautiously to modest-budget film ventures. General Electric started its Tomorrow Productions in December 1970 and announced plans to make two films a year with budgets up to $3 million. Bristol-Myers entered the field by acquiring Palomar Pictures, but most newcomers started up their own operations. Xerox announced plans to make thirteen children's features, three for release in 1971. Mattel commissioned *Sounder,* a film starring Kevin Hooks as the son in a black family on a depression-era Louisiana farm.

But the MPAA had other problems besides corporate competition (which resulted in the takeover by conglomerates of Paramount, Universal, and United Artists). In 1968, a code of four letters had been devised by the Motion Picture Association of America as a guide to moviegoers. Films had begun to experiment with nudity, sex and profanity, and this system was intended to warn those who might consider such material unsuitable, and also to prevent government-imposed censorship. A Code and Rating Administration viewed each film and rated it before it was released to the public.

By 1971 simulated sex, total nudity from any angle, and virtually all the language of the street had reached the screen. In May the Film Commission of the National Council of Churches and the Catholic Office for Motion Pictures announced withdrawal of their support of the MPAA ratings, which they termed "unreliable." The eleven-member board that reviewed the films had been challenged periodically by filmmakers and studios, and sometimes this board had backed down and given films a more "favorable" rating. The two Catholic organizations cited several films in which they felt bad taste had reached an extreme.

Heston and Valenti stood by the ratings despite the unexpected attack. But M-G-M, a charter member of the

MPAA, also resigned; it called the code "confusing and impractical." It returned to the fold a few weeks later, but other controversies (including the Van Peebles suit) continued to pop up during the next two years.

This was just another thorn in Hollywood's side. There had been little improvement since the code had been in effect. Only three companies made profits in 1970, and the biggest loser, Twentieth Century-Fox, had a deficit of $102 million in the two years. Things continued to look bad; of the 100 motion pictures under way in the spring of 1971, 30 were being made by independent producers away from Hollywood sound stages.

Not until mid-1972 did the industry show signs of recovery. M-G-M and National General were in better financial condition, and production, boosted largely by those thriving competitive independents, whose films they distributed profitably, began to rise. Only a year later, Columbia remained the sole studio still operating in the fiscal red.

"Runaways" (as Hollywood calls movies made abroad by American companies) were the chief cause of Hollywood unemployment, which rose over sixty percent in at least one union of the Hollywood Film Council. At one point in 1971 there were thirty-five runaways in production. The trend seemed likely to continue, since foreign governments were offering generous subsidies to attract increasingly cost-conscious producers. There was a boom in Italy during the summer. Even Charlton Heston made a film in Spain.

Hollywood was also suffering from a cutback in television series production, which in 1971 accounted for most of the work on studio lots. Films for television, the largest source of screen actors' incomes, were also cut back. Many stars facing unemployment had found temporary solutions in TV. When the 1971 fall shows premiered, there were eighteen major stars—from Glenn Ford to Shirley Mac-Laine—in television series, receiving bountiful salaries for each segment. Public reaction, reflected in Nielsen ratings, was disappointing. Programs died after one season; some did not last that long.

To what extent is television experience helpful for black film artists? Some, like Bill Cosby, who started on television, were able to move on to films. Others, who, like Diahann Carroll, proved themselves in film, were able to win starring roles on television series. Successful performers were able to work in both media. Some progress was made in the directing of network shows. Among the noted directors were Emmy-Award-winning Mark Warren (of "Laugh-In") and actor Ivan Dixon who, with Sid McCoy and Luther James, were black directors on "The Bill Cosby Show" and "Julia."

The first prime-time television movie with a black theme was *The Sheriff*, with Ossie Davis, Ruby Dee, and Kyle Johson. In this story, the son of a black sheriff in the South faces a serious decision when his girlfriend is raped by a white man. The undistinguished formula drama was released in 1970, followed by three black-oriented television films in 1971, and four more in 1972.

But how have blacks been affected in their struggle for recognition in the movie industry? In Hollywood films, blacks advanced from small typecast roles to major-character portrayals. They began to occupy directors' chairs and organize their own production companies.

Though on a comparatively small scale, there were

black efforts to control film production from script through distribution. The major studios do not hold a monopoly on the release of motion pictures, but TAM and Cinemethics International are still the only black companies specifically organized to release feature films. William Greaves Productions does have a releasing arm, but until now it has been used exclusively for Greaves productions. While film distribution is more than a matter of shipping prints to one movie house in each city, it is probable that there will be others like TAM, handling only black productions, within five years.

Potential profits from black communities had not been overlooked by white investors, who were reaping their shares from movies already circulating. It was estimated that blacks were spending $110 million annually on movies. About twelve hundred movie houses were in predominantly black neighborhoods. In addition, more blacks were going "downtown" to see first-run movies (especially those with black-oriented themes and black casts), and they were not frightened away by higher admission fees.

The black audience, which has been estimated to be as high as fifty-three percent of the total by the film industry, is becoming increasingly important for another reason. Black people are a young people (census figures show that sixty-seven percent of the black population is under thirty-five), and it is young people—black and white—who account for seventy-five percent of film audiences.

In general, film distributors ruled that films with black appeal should open in downtown areas. When *Right On*, a dramatic visualization of the Last Poets of Harlem, was released in 1971 by Concept East New York Ltd., two black filmmakers attempted to buck the trend.

Producer Woody King, Jr. turned down distribution offers from United Artists and Universal to show what could
be done by appealing directly to the black audience.
King had described the film as being "totally black," making no concessions in language or symbolism to white
audiences. Its non-narrative approach in covering a day in
Harlem would interest Third World audiences, King said.
Its combination of pop culture and relevance was the key-
note that the major studios had missed in trying to pitch
their products to blacks.

Right On had won the International Film Critics Prize
and the Interfilm Award at the 1970 Mannheim Festival,
and after test screenings in Washington, Atlanta, and Dayton, and a turnaway midnight engagement in New York,
King and his director, Herbert Danska, were sure they
had a winner.

In promoting the film, King had taken fewer of the
customary daily newspaper ads, concentrating on spots
over New York's soul radio stations and relying heavily
on posters, flyers, and leaflets to reach nighborhood audiences directly and more effectively. *Right On* was previewed in Harlem, and it opened in theaters on the West
Side. It attracted a large black audience at first, but business was slow after the first week.

The intentions of the two filmmakers were admirable,
but their failure in judgment revealed important facts. One
was that blacks (like most weekend movie audiences) respond poorly to "message" films in commercial theaters.
Another was that blacks enjoy leaving their communities to go "downtown" and be entertained in style.

In New York City thirty-five theaters present Latin-
oriented films to a Spanish-speaking population of less

than one million. Theaters in communities of two million blacks do not approach that number. Only four serve Harlem and one (the Apollo) specializes in live entertainment rather than first-run films.

An attempt to increase the number failed. Westown Theater, a Walter Reade project to test the practicality of theaters in black neighborhoods, opened in Dayton in September, 1970. It closed in March, 1971, a financial loss.

The theater had been the first of several planned by the chain for black-patronized shopping centers. However, a spokesman for the company said, "The theater never made money, and black people never supported it. Our losses were drastic. Some nights we played to three or four persons. We opened with an exclusive first run of Avco Embassy's *Soldier Blue,* and spent more on advertising than we took in at the box office."

But what would have happened if the theater had played an obviously black-oriented film like *Cotton Comes to Harlem,* even in re-release?

A government report showed that nearly half of the nation's black population was concentrated in fifty cities, with one-third in fifteen. As a result of migration and growth, six cities had black majorities, and the population in eight others was forty or more percent black. With black-oriented businesses becoming more numerous, there would inevitably be more black shopping centers like the one in Dayton.

In 1972 the number of black-owned film theaters across the country was about fifteen. In Chicago, the city with the nation's second largest black population, there was open discontent in the black community, since only three of one hundred eighty downtown theaters were owned or leased by blacks. The protests produced some improvement. In Buffalo, the Apollo was renovated after a six-year shutdown owing to a fire. When it reopened with an "Afro-American motif, zebra-skin walls, and a black-and-gold color scheme in carpeting and seating," the 700-seat house booked *The Lost Man* on a bill with *The Beguiled,* starring Clint Eastwood. Raymond Moss, the theater's new owner, announced that he would book features directed by, or presenting, black talent.

There is a weekly trade magazine called *Box Office.* Within its pages a crucial problem of the industry is discussed—for it is at the movie houses (initially, at least) that films succeed or fail. When Hollywood is in financial pain, there is an ache in the more than 14,000 theaters across the country. Owners have been forced to come up with independent schemes for staying open in hard times.

In Los Angeles, for example, organ music filled one theater as popular silent era stars cavorted on the screen. New York theaters ran simultaneous revivals of the films of Buster Keaton, Charlie Chaplin, and the Marx Brothers. In Dallas, the Capri Theater offered ten films in seven separate auditoriums. *Box Office* reported that of the 413 indoor theaters built in 1970, 210 were of the multi-auditorium style.

Owing to the steady decrease in the number of new films, exhibitors played and replayed successful movies like *Love Story* and *The Graduate.* Drive-in theaters tried a development called Prismalite, which made it possible for them to show films in daylight.

Some New York-area theaters experimented with the one-dollar admission fee—a popular practice in previous decades—just as President Nixon was announcing his own economic controls.

Century Theaters reduced prices at its forty-four Showcase Theaters from the $1.50 to $3.00 range to 50 cents during the week and a weekend top of $2.00. Associated Independent Theaters lowered adult tickets in nine houses to $1.50, with Saturday admission $2.00. Twelve of their twenty-six other theaters were already charging a dollar during the week and $1.50 on Saturdays. Soon more than 100 one-dollar houses were in operation, and skeptics like Loew's Theaters were watching the results closely.

The program was especially successful in some New York suburbs, where the goal was to attract middle-income patrons, and the reduced fee was usually offered with a program of inoffensive but popular family-oriented films.

Black audiences were ardently courted by theater owners in 1971. By the final week of August New York City theaters were in obvious competition for the soul dollar, particularly at the Times Square Cinerama, DeMille, Forum, Penthouse, and Victoria theaters. At 42nd Street movie houses, *Shaft*, at the Lyric, played across the street from *Sweetback*, at the Harris, and only a few doors down from Sidney Poitier's *Brother John*, at the Selvyn. Up Broadway near 47th Street, the Cinerama Theater showed *Black Jesus. Soul to Soul* was at the DeMille on the same block. Two blocks uptown, the Trans Lux West also played *Shaft*. On the east side, near 34th Street, the Murray Hill Theater had *Black Jesus*. The Beekman, on 65th Street, showed *Soul to Soul,* and *Shaft* was at the 72nd Street Playhouse.

Just below Harlem (at the Olympia), it was *Cotton Comes to Harlem* and *Putney Swope*. In Harlem *Shaft* was teamed with Jim Brown in *tick tick tick* (at the Loew's Victoria) on 125th Street, and *Dark of the Sun* (at the Roosevelt) on Seventh Avenue near 145th Street. By the end of the week six features with Jim Brown were being shown including the two above, *El Condor, The Dirty Dozen, The Grasshopper*, and 100 *Rifles. The Landlord* and *The Learning Tree* were playing in other parts of the city. On Wednesday *Sweetback* was uptown, (at the RKO) near 181st Street, and downtown (RKO 23rd Cinema). As Labor Day weekend approached, *Cabin in the Sky, The Dutchman, If He Hollers Let Him Go,* and *The McMasters* were re-released. There had been other black double features; in March, *Cotton* and *They Call Me Mister Tibbs,* and in July, *Riot* and *Uptight.*

It was not long before the media took notice. In September, *Newsweek* ran a full-page article, "The Black Movie Boom." The industry had been calling the 1971 summer the worst in box office history, *Newsweek* said. Black films appeared to be the only consistently popular attractions in a season of sporadic individual successes.

In *Variety* the article "Black Pix and White Market: True Trend or Just Novelty?" concluded from the success of *Sweetback* and *Shaft* that black audiences favored black characters who beat The Man and the system. *The Great White Hope* was cited by a number of black people interviewed as less successful, because the hero "lost in the end."

In the following months, *Time,* the *New York Daily News, Life, Cue* the *New York Times,* and even network television had features on the "black film boom."

The beginning of a black film industry had been established. Many formerly skeptical producers were convinced that black audiences were potential sources of twice as much profit as the once trend-setting youth market, and that blacks could keep films "in the black," making money.

Addison Verrill of *Variety* summed up: "Whether the black feature bonanza has peaked or not, it is clear that over the past year the industry has recognized, and will be made to recognize in the future, a heretofore ignored segment of the filmgoing population that has the coin and is willing to spend it. For indie (independent) distribs happy with a limited but respectable return (and the full potential of the black market has yet to be determined), that may be the answer. But the majors are still looking for the film that will attract the full audience spectrum and thus make up for a number of losers in one fell swoop."

The full impact of black productions was still to come. Which films blacks flocked to see still depended largely on white decisions. Despite the box office power of films like *Shaft*, only a small percentage of new films were black-oriented. In 1970 they numbered fourteen out of about four hundred major films and only increased to seventeen the following year. By 1972 over fifty had been made in that three-year period, and fewer than five were independent black productions. Painful as the figures were for blacks in the industry, it seemed for a time that no one else cared.

14

Black Production Companies: A New Independence

When the recession hit Hollywood in the late 1960s, independent companies emerged to fill the void caused by cutbacks in production at the big studios. Comparatively inexpensive "now" productions like *Easy Rider* (which cost $370,000 and grossed more than $50,000,000 by 1971) became spectacular hits.

The recession was not the only reason for the advent of independent movies. Many young filmmakers wanted to make films without interference from studio executives, whose control had forced even many veteran directors to complain.

A variety of circumstances, including the popularity of television, caused movie audiences to dwindle. In 1971 only 17.5 million Americans attended a movie a week compared with a peak 80 million in 1946. In the same period, Hollywood film production had fallen from 378 to 143 pictures a year. Over 500 films had been made in 1937. Income dropped correspondingly; gross box office receipts were down twenty-five percent over the previous quarter-century even though admission prices had tripled in those years. The studios were losing millions of dollars apiece.

Audiences were younger—and blacker—and adjustment was necessary for economic survival, since only one out of six movies was making a profit. The studios were forced to view their procedures and try to recover.

An important goal of black production companies was to train more blacks for off-camera jobs. Certain motion picture unions were overwhelming obstacles to black film-makers. A frequent charge was that some of the 254 unions accepted blacks only on a token basis. In 1968 and 1969 film and television studios increased the number of blacks in production jobs by forty-eight percent, but even then the number of blacks in production was less than five percent of the total.

An example of the need for blacks in post-filming phases of production was presented by Brock Peters, who had starred in *The McMasters,* the story of a black ex-soldier, romantically involved with an Indian girl, who returns to his home town and a series of racial confrontations.

Peters wrote to the Screen Actors Guild in the summer of 1970 requesting that his name be removed from all screen credits and advertising on the Chevron Pictures release. He claimed that the British backers had played up the scene where he raped the Indian girl, but had cut seven minutes showing the remorse felt by the character, Benjie McMasters, over his act.

"The cuts dehumanize the character I created and move it close to a brutish unpalatable stereotype," the actor complained. "My integrity as a responsible artist is challenged in the edited version. It is demeaning to me as an actor and a black man."

Peters was joined in his protest by Harold Jacob Smith, the film's scriptwriter, who also petitioned the Writers Guild of America to have his name removed from all screen credits and ads. Both versions were exhibited in American theaters, but for Peters, a half-victory was no victory at all.

Because of such situations, well-known blacks had followed Van Peebles's lead, organizing individual production companies to gain greater control over all stages of their future projects.

Sidney Poitier organized E & R Productions and later, Verdon Productions. *The Lost Man* and subsequent films had crews in which nearly fifty percent were blacks and other minority group members.

The Angel Levine was made by Harry Belafonte Enterprises, which also produced *Odds Against Tomorrow* in 1959 and *Island in the Sun* in 1957. During the New York filming of *Levine* (in which he starred), Belafonte trained fifteen black and Puerto Rican apprentices at camera-side in a program financed by the Ford Foundation.

In 1965 Sammy Davis, Jr.'s Trace-Mark Productions had developed and produced *A Man Called Adam.*

Bill Cosby, whose comedy record albums helped win him a dramatic role in "I Spy" and later his own television show, came into movies with his own production company, Jemmin, Inc. *Man and Boy* was Cosby's first feature film. It told of the struggles of a black family on the frontier, with emphasis on the father-son relationship. The film was G-rated, aimed at family audiences. Cosby headed an impressive cast that included Gloria Foster, Yaphet Kotto, Douglas Turner Ward, and a gifted child actor, George Spell. Before *Man and Boy* was released, Cosby announced plans for a second project, an anti-drug film called *The Candy Man,* which never materialized.

Previews for *Man and Boy* were held in northern California in the spring of 1971, and a fall opening in Chicago was announced. But Cosby encountered problems with the only studio interested in his film when he insisted that the villain, a horse thief, be black. The studio's view was that bigger box office reaction would be generated by a black-white conflict.

Cosby, who had loaned Melvin Van Peebles $50,000 to complete *Sweet Sweetback's Badasssss Song,* was fortunately able to begin production of *Man and Boy* with his own money. When costs reached $450,000, however, even he needed backing. He received $880,000 from J. Douglas Crean, the millionaire founder of a California-based mobile home firm, and the picture was completed.

Cosby had told a *Chicago Tribune* interviewer, "In feature films, it's like Jackie Robinson time. In order for me or any other black director to make a feature, our first film has to make it big. I've got to steal second, third, and home plate. We're not allowed the luxury of being human.

"The day when there will be a black movie premiering in a black theater and being reviewed by a black critic is a long way off," he admitted. "But we can't be worried about that. Henry Ford didn't wait until there was a freeway system to start building his automobiles. The studios must be convinced that black movies can make money." Cosby suggested that there was a better chance for black films on television, where production costs—and attendant risks—are smaller.

By autumn, promotion of *Man and Boy* in trade journals had begun, and a distributor (Levitt-Pickman) had released the film in Baltimore and Detroit. Cosby appeared on "The Dick Cavett Show" for a ninety-minute interview to publicize the film. But audience response was not encouraging, and the picture disappeared quietly. On March 15, 1972, again without fanfare, *Man and Boy* arrived in New York for a showcase run that included screenings at the 125th Street Apollo. Poor reviews and tepid audience reaction greeted the film, which ran for only one week.

Jemmin remained on the West Coast, but Cosby moved east and became involved in other ventures, while also taking graduate courses at the University of Massachusetts. In February, his Jemmin-produced television drama, "To All My Friends On Shore," drew critical applause. Filmed on location in Norwalk, Connecticut, it was a contemporary tale about a struggling black family, similar in many ways to *Man and Boy* (which might have fared better on television). Cosby decided to return to television for his second show that fall.

In 1970 a group of young blacks got together in Compton, California, hoping to make their community a part of the motion picture industry. Compton, a middle-class residential city of 75,000 ten miles south of Los Angeles, is noted for its junior college and its almost exclusively black population. This group formed a production company called K-Calb (spell it backwards). With their screenplay *The Bus Is Coming*, and $30,000 of an estimated $175,000 budget, they began shooting. Just over a year later, with 14,000 feet of film in the can (seventy-five percent of the picture), the company was broke.

Horace Jackson, who had written and produced the picture, went to local banks for help. He was advised to seek out wealthy blacks like Sammy Davis, Jr. and Sidney Poitier for further financing. Asked if he had approached the Hollywood studios for money, Jackson said in a *Variety* interview, "As for the majors, we can't get to their doors. I take that back. We did get in to see one who said that if we'd put somebody like Tina Turner in the picture, they might be interested."

The day after the *Variety* article appeared, the film was revived. A new distributor recently arrived from the Midwest, William Thompson, gave K-Calb the funds it needed. He also guaranteed its release and offered to help in the promotion. The film was completed, and plans for a summer release were announced.

Thirty-eight-year-old Jackson had come to California as a young man with seventeen dollars in his pocket, one suitcase, and a determination to see movie stars. He began working for a Baptist church in the Los Angeles area, and managed to collect enough talented people to make *Living Between Two Worlds,* the story of a black man torn between jazz and the pulpit. It was put together for only $10,000, most of which was borrowed from friends. It earned much more, but unfortunately not for Jackson.

While attending Los Angeles City College for three years and working as a recreation director for the city schools, Jackson wrote the script for *Bus.* When minority hiring came into vogue in Hollywood, he got a job as a music cutter's apprentice at Paramount.

"My work consisted of carrying film reels back and

forth between offices on a bike," he told a *Los Angeles Times* interviewer.

Instead of taking Van Peebles's path to artistic independence, K-Calb preferred to join the Hollywood family of filmmakers. Jackson chose to sign with the International Alliance of Theatrical Stage Employees and tried (at first unsuccessfully) to make a total deferment deal with the Screen Actors Guild.

With all the uncertainty and pressure behind (he and his family had even been evicted from their home when an eighty-five-dollar payment was not made), Jackson awaited public reaction to his film. It premiered at the Hollywood Palladium as a benefit for the Danny Thomas charity, Saint Jude's Hospital, in Memphis, Tennessee.

The population in Compton is seventy-one percent black. It was a perfect setting for the film, which told the story of a black Vietnam veteran who returns home for the funeral of his brother, a civil rights activist slain by a racist cop.

The Bus Is Coming was selected for showing at the 1971 San Francisco Film Festival in October. The film's director was Wendell James Franklin, the first black man to become (in 1962) a member of the Director's Guild of America. Franklin's first film was following in the tradition set by Melvin Van Peebles with *The Story of a Three Day Pass,* four years earlier. Unlike Van Peebles, Franklin did not come away a surprise winner of the festival, but like Van Peebles's film *Sweetback, Bus* became the target of ridicule by some activists. With inexperienced actors and actresses and a low budget, technical perfection could not have been expected of the fledgling director. His more vocal detractors, who laughed and booed during the showing, were dissatisfied with the story, which ended optimistically.

When Franklin appeared onstage after the screening, a group of hecklers crowded to the front, yelling obscenities and characterizing the film as being representative of Hollywood's values. Amid the taunts, Franklin, who began his career as an NBC parking lot attendant, answered, "I was making a motion picture, not a social comment. You don't realize how difficult it has been for blacks in Hollywood. One has to get started somehow. The ultimate goal should be money and employment for our people in the industry. Every black story I see is a bring-down. I want to bring people up."

But the box office tally was an indicator many respected. *Bus* grossed $77,000 that week, beating *Shaft* after only two weeks of distribution. And when the film reached New York a few weeks later, it drew well despite overwhelmingly poor reviews.

The film was to gross nearly $4 million before international distribution, but there was concern over the slow returns from a sub-distributor, Hip Productions, since salaries for cast, crew and labs had all been deferred in a budget that had escalated to $230,000. As a new company, K-Calb was paying its learning dues to distributor and exhibitor who made unhappy magic with numbers—always at the expense of the filmmaker.

"We're continuing our filmmaking," Franklin announced from the new K-Calb offices at the Sam Goldwyn Studios in Hollywood. "Just like all the other companies, we plan to put out two or three films a year."

Jackson, now president of K-Calb, said the company had begun a new film, *Spirit in Darkness,* an "epic" story of former slaves traveling by wagon train to new lives in the North. This time stars like William Marshall, Beah Richards, Juanita Moore, and Mantan Moreland were involved. And in a move counter to the trend, K-Calb hired a white director, eighty-one-year-old George Marshall, to bring his expertise to their second effort.

Although *The Bus Is Coming* was not a critical success, it was a winner with the black audience. It ranked as the most significant effort of any new group in 1971, proving that community films could be made.

On Friday, July 2, 1971, another movie, billed as "the first major black motion picture," premiered at the Santa Monica Auditorium. *Black Chariot* had been made independently for the modest sum of $125,000 with writing, production, and direction by Robert L. Goodwin.

The forty-four-year-old Californian had begun his career in 1948, writing and producing several plays. He went on to create fifty hours of drama for the three major television networks, including scripts for series like "Bonanza," "Julia," "Love American Style," "Insight," "The Outcasts," "And Then Came Bronson," and "Dundee and the Culhane." He also wrote two scripts for movies, one for the Mirisch Brothers and the other for Dick Clark Productions.

In 1970 he set up Robert L. Goodwin Productions. Bypassing banks and major studios, he mailed letters describing his background and soliciting investment in his film to black professionals in Los Angeles. He also asked for help from blacks in the industry, including performers who had acted in his television plays.

In the professional group, only four doctors, a dentist, a lawyer, and a rabbi responded. Of the blacks in the movie industry, answers came from Bernie Casey (who starred in *Black Chariot*), Diahann Carroll, Barbara Mc-Nair, William Marshall, and Madie Norman.

Goodwin was forced to look elsewhere. He took his proposal to friends (including Bill Greaves) and the community. Ninety-five percent of the eventual backers were black, many with shares of $50 or less. A minimum of $5 or four Blue Chip stamp books could be invested. Goodwin estimated that about $5,000 came from the Blue Chip stamps. The film also received substantial support from the Black Muslims.

"I started collecting money in June 1970," Goodwin said, "finishing the script as I was going."

Critical reaction was uniformly negative, emphasizing the production's technical deficiencies, but plans for world-wide distribution were (prematurely) announced. An advertisement notified the public that new investments would be accepted for the next ninety days. A second film, *Roscoe,* never got off the ground, and *Black Chariot* did not even reach its anticipated audience. Distribution problems limited screenings to the West Coast, and the project appeared to be one of the few failures in the growth of the new black-produced films. Then an entirely new premiere was held in August 1973 which was co-sponsored by a group called Third World Distributors. At a glance, Goodwin's tenacity seemed to match his resourcefulness.

By the late 1960s many blacks had turned their attention to off-camera jobs. And help eventually came from a not-always-so-cooperative federal government. Early in 1970, Attorney General John Mitchell announced agreement between the Justice Department and representatives of the motion picture industry, the three major television networks, and the craft unions to facilitate more representative minority hiring. The agreement was reached after two months of conferences, which followed a 1969 investigation by the Equal Employment Opportunity Commission in Los Angeles.

Specifically, the plan called for the establishment of a minority pool for craft jobs; permanent craft jobs to be based on a twenty percent ratio of minority to white members; referral for daily craft employment to be at a specified ratio of minority pool personnel to general labor now on the roster; and finally, a program aimed at training minority group members for complicated craft jobs. Seventy-three motion picture producers, their nine craft union locals, the International Alliance of Theatrical Stage Employees, and the Association of Motion Picture and Television Producers signed the agreement.

A year later, the agreement became the focal point in a campaign to unseat the business manager of one of the participating unions. Local 44 of the IATSE Propmen, led by Allen Hill, openly attempted to remove Milton Olson. Hill, who termed the Justice Department plans "outrageous," was one of six co-chairmen on a committee opposing the minority program. A twenty-five-year member of the local, Hill was drafted by petition to run against Olson in the spring election.

Hill publicly charged that officers of the union local had not voted with "intelligence" when they accepted the program, and asserted that they did not have the "guts" to fight Richard Walsh, IATSE's international president at the time of the agreement. Hill claimed the program was hurting white union members and driving producers from Hollywood to places like New York, Chicago, and Miami, where they were not bound by agreement to accept untrained personnel. Contending that Local 44 had already been hit hard, he charged that there would be even less work in Hollywood unless the agreement was thrown out.

The training program had been operating since August 3, 1970, and in June of the following year, the first two of thirty-five trainees graduated from the Grips Minority Training Program and went on to guaranteed forty-hour jobs as grips at Universal Studios. While in training, Edward Martinez and John Mettles had been paid by the Association of Motion Picture and Television Producers, with costs reimbursed through the Contract Services Administration Trust Fund.

In November, however, a group calling itself IATSE Group for Union Equality filed suit against the Department of Justice, the Association of Motion Picture and Television Producers, and individual producers. The suit was heard after a federal judge denied a motion by the Justice Department and the producers' group to throw the challenge out of court. However, it was revealed that the unions of cameramen, soundmen, costumers, and film editors had reached the required level of minority hiring by the set deadline.

In 1971 minority representation became one of the many issues in the first contested election in the Screen Actors Guild's thirty-eight-year history. Bert Freed led an independent ticket that included Beah Richards, challenging the 20,000-member guild's official nominee, John Gavin. The independent platform called for establishment of minority and women's caucuses. Freed said the guild was the only union in the entertainment business without such representation.

Charlton Heston, who had served six one-year terms as president, asserted that the charge of improper minority representation was "racist slander." He said, "I, particularly, bitterly resent this charge. Before I took office, there were board members who were Chinese, black, Indian, and Mexican, at a time when other unions didn't have members of these races."

When the ballots were counted, the official slate had won twice as many votes as the independents. But four months later an Ethnic Minorities Committee was established by the guild's board of directors to work on minority projects. Robert DoQui was named chairman of the five-member group. The committee was expected to seek the participation of black, Mexican, Asian American, and American Indian communities.

Union membership rules resulted in the organization of the Black Stuntmen's Association. Ernie Robinson, head of the group, explained: "There were, before we organized, maybe two or three blacks in the whole profession. This was out of a total of some seventy-five or so. The guild, the Stuntmen's Association, excluded blacks and other minorities by requiring that they earn at least $10,000. Now very few blacks could get work to begin with. So how could we qualify for the guild?"

Marvin Walters, one of the group's co-founders, told how a chance meeting on the Universal Studios lot in 1968 led to the group's formation. "I met a guy named Eddie Smith, who said that he had been trying to start a black stuntmen's association since 1966. He said that no one seemed to be interested. Somehow, through the Justice

Department, he had gotten his union card. He was important to the group later on because he knew a lot of the pitfalls and directed us away from them. At first we had a lot of problems with the white stuntmen's association, but when they saw we were really going to stick, a lot of their guys came out and gave us pointers on how to do different things. Since 1968 it's been going pretty well. Now some of our men are making as high as $35,000 a year."

With blacks getting more acting parts, whites had been performing stunts (in blackface) that logically should have gone to blacks. The black stuntmen had been hampered by lack of experience in what was a lucrative but often dangerous profession. All were former athletes, and all spent considerable time perfecting their techniques. In 1970 there were twenty-eight men and two women in the group.

A victory was won in the spring of 1971. After meeting with Warner Brothers, Cherokee Productions, the NAACP, the Screen Actors Guild, and the Equal Employment Opportunity Commission, Warner Brothers ruled that the practice of hiring white stuntmen to double in blackface for black actors and extras would cease.

Guidelines governing future productions were announced. Employment of black stuntmen would not be limited to doubling for black actors. Blacks would be included in all scenes requiring general stuntwork. Stuntmen would allow qualified black stuntmen to observe set-ups of stunts on sets, with the objective of assisting them to become gaffers. Warner Brothers would make its facilities available and have stunt specialists help black stuntmen to improve their skills.

In 1965 thirty-five men began meeting twice weekly to train as a new "Tenth Cavalry." They organized to re-create the historic all-black cavalry units that operated in the West after the Civil War and remained active until 1944. The group appeared in a "High Chaparral" television segment, "The Buffalo Soldiers," and made its screen debut in a parade sequence in *Hello Dolly*. Screenwriter Samuel A. Peeples had been assigned to develop a film script about the group for Paramount. The project was also to include the Black Stuntmen's Association.

A movie called *The Red, White and Black* opened in California early in 1971 amid internal controversy. Len Glascow, president of the Tenth Cavalry, explained to *Soul* that his group had planned to do a film and television series patterned after the exploits of the original post-Civil War troops. At the suggestion of a friend, he contacted a white lawyer, Harry Weed, in March 1969. Weed offered to be their business manager but declined to sign a formal contract "until they started making money."

In October, Glascow received a phone call from Larry Long. Long was the producer-director on a Ford Foundation project putting up $225,000 for documentaries about blacks during the settlement of the West. The series was to be called "The Black Frontier." Long wanted to base one segment on the Buffalo Soldiers of the Tenth Cavalry. Glascow turned over negotiations for the project to Weed, along with partial payment for his service. (A second installment was due on arrival in El Paso, Texas, location for the documentary.)

Unknown to the Tenth, Weed set up a company, Dakota Productions, and arranged with Larry Long to make, in addition to the documentary, a movie version of the

Buffalo Soldiers story. The Tenth had been committed to work for Dakota Productions for a small salary plus only five percent of the profits—after cost, according to *Soul.*

The Tenth retained a black lawyer and filed suit against Weed for fraud and misrepresentation. They also withdrew from the film, followed by the Black Stuntmen's Association, Woody Strode, and actor John Russell. Other black members of the cast, Robert DoQui, Lincoln Kilpatrick, Isaac Fields, Rafer Johnson, Janee Michelle, and Isabel Stanford, remained, caught in an awkward situation.

In the meantime, Weed had turned over rights to the film to producers James Northern and Stuart Hirschman because they had poured so much money into an attempt to keep the project afloat.

DoQui, who had a starring role, found himself at odds with the producers and the white director, John Cardos. In a post-filming interview with *Soul's* Walter Burrell, he admitted, "I can see the inconsistencies in the script. I can see the flaws in the direction. But believe me, we had a hell of a fight to get what we got. There are a hell of a lot of things to knock in this movie. But there is also some good too, and that can't simply be buried."

According to Chamba Productions there were at least fifteen production companies in 1970. Charles Green, producer-director and head of Trans-Oceanic Productions, was the first black admitted to the Independent Motion Picture Producers Association in Hollywood. Green said it was still easier, even in the seventies, for his company to get financing abroad. He was negotiating a five-picture deal in Spain at the time. "The area is wide open for blacks," he said, "but they have got to forget Hollywood."

On the East Coast, Ossie Davis had done just that. During the winter of 1970 he announced the formation of Third World Cinema Corporation, designed to provide opportunities for minority group actors and technical crews. At this time there were still few blacks in the technical area of the industry. The U. S. Manpower Career and Development Administration allocated $200,-000 for payment of trainees while learning and earning union cards. At a press conference in the offices of New York's Economic Development Administration, Davis said that the goals of the corporation were "to produce, in New York City, films and documentaries utilizing talents and providing jobs for blacks, Puerto Ricans, and other minority groups, and to distribute them to motion picture houses and television."

Davis said, "Box office receipts on recent films done by and about blacks have indicated a substantial black audience throughout the country. The audience should have an equal opportunity to participate in the profits."

Plans were announced for a biography of blues singer Billie Holiday, starring Diana Sands (a Third World board member). Ironically, Motown Records, which had just organized a film and television production arm, announced a similar project—pre-budgeted at $5 million—that would present their super songstress Diana Ross in a screen debut.

Like Third World, Motown planned other projects besides feature films. But films were good showcases for Motown's artists. Marvin Gaye, a Motown performer for years, made his dramatic debut as a former Green Beret turned motorcyclist in American International's *Chrome and Hot Leather.* A few months later he wrote his first score for Twentieth Century-Fox's *Trouble Man.* Michael Jackson, lead singer of The Jackson Five, sang his first movie score (for *Ben*) at age thirteen.

Starting from a row of modest stores on West Grand Boulevard in Detroit, Motown had blossomed into perhaps the greatest commercial success story in modern music. Year after year the company introduced new artists and top hits that sold and made millions. The acts were professionally managed and maintained a popularity virtually unheard of in the unpredictable youth market. With writers like Smokey Robinson, Motown turned out a style of soul that attracted turnaway crowds at Harlem's Apollo and also drew raves from the big spenders in Las Vegas nightclubs. Television variety shows used Motown stars frequently, groups continued to perform even when individual members left, and those who chose the solo route also fared well.

It was not long before Hollywood lured president Berry Gordy, Jr., Miss Ross, and Gaye to the West Coast. Offices were set up and plans were made for a series of television specials, a cartoon show, and movies. The new arm of the company was called Motown Productions. The staff soon increased from three to over a hundred people.

The Billie Holiday story was to be produced by Jay Weston. Paramount signed to release it. *Lady Sings the Blues* marked Motown's entry into feature film production. The question of who would re-create the life of the famous singer had become a countrywide controversy. Louis McKay, Billie's husband, maintained that he alone owned rights to the story, and that he had agreed to let Motown make the film. In New York, Ossie Davis argued that "the star's life is in the public domain," and said he would continue with his project. McKay threatened to sue Third World if they went on with their movie. Third World nevertheless scheduled a July 15 casting call, and chose John Berry to direct their version. Diana Ross gave birth to a daughter in August. Diana Sands had just completed *Georgia, Georgia* in Sweden. By late September, pre-filming preparation for both versions was in progress.

Reaction in the black community ranged from doubt to consternation at the news that Miss Ross would portray Billie Holiday. But when the film was fiinished, Hollywood rumors predicted that the film and Miss Ross would surprise everyone. By then Motown had a suite of offices at the Paramount studios, and Gordy had signed Miss Ross's co-star, Billie Dee Williams, to a multi-picture contract. Joe Porter, Motown's Coordinator of Theatrical Affairs, said, "Quality film is an issue in itself. We're going to try and make damn good movies. We want high quality products."

In New York, the Third World production still had not gotten off the ground. In the training area, however, the company was active. In 1971 the Directors Guild of New York agreed to allow twenty-five minority group trainees to work for an eighteen-month period on Third World films. At that time, Davis would allow five or more candidates to continue in the Guild's own training program for another six months of study.

Wardell Gaynor, administrator of Third World's on-the-job training program, said, "The OJT is working. For example, we've put six people through the program who have passed the exam for projectionists. We have trainees working on the sequels to both *Shaft* and *Cotton Comes to Harlem,* as well as in the commercial houses and on some documentaries being filmed in New York. Most of them will go into the IA or NABET when they complete their apprenticeships."

Ossie Davis later disclosed that Third World had agreed to give a forty percent interest in the company to a community-based group (unnamed) to qualify for a $400,000 federal Model Cities grant.

Third World also said it had signed a contract with Twentieth Century-Fox to distribute their five planned films over the next three years. By this time, priority had been changed. *Thunder,* an original screenplay by John O. Killens, was now at the top of the list. But even that changed. In a late August press conference attended by Mayor Lindsay, production of a comedy-drama called *Claudine* was announced. When shooting finally began September 6 (after two delays to make cutting changes), Third World Cinema actually entered the world of feature film production.

Georgia, Georgia opened in New York in the spring of 1972. In the era of black "firsts," it was a feature film with a black theme, made by a black producer in Europe. Jack Jordan's publicly owned Kelly-Jordan Enterprises was responsible for this film, which was based on Maya Angelou's first screenplay.

Jack Jordan's partner was Irish, but the company's films were black. Diana Sands starred in *Georgia, Georgia,* the story of the identity problem of a popular black singer on tour in Europe. It was not an exceptional film, but it was the first recent film with a black woman in the central role, and there were a few bright and meaningful moments.

After *Georgia, Georgia* opened, Jordan moved his operation to New York. He had an exclusive contract to film
all of James Baldwin's literary works, and Baldwin would
even direct one, *The Inheritance.* Maya Angelou was pre-
paring to direct her first film, an adaptation of her auto-
biography, *I Know Why a Caged Bird Sings.* Kelly-Jordan
also planned to produce *Ganja and Hess,* written and directed by Bill Gunn, whom Jordan called "the black Stanley Kubrick." All the Kelly-Jordan films would be produced and shot in Europe and marketed in the United
States, increasing the margin for profit, assuming a distributor could be found.

"It's going to take ten years," Jordan said, "for blacks
to have the expertise to build their own communications
industry. But it will come eventually."

Young black directors and producers continued to look
to the community for the financing of meaningful films.
Some had bad experiences with white banks. Others were
ideologically opposed to continued dependence on whites.
With grass roots support, the newcomers hoped to bring
added revenue to ghetto areas by the use of local residents
in the production and distribution of their films.

These new black directors and producers were encouraged by the shift to low-budget movies. They believed
undiscovered talent abounded in Harlem, Watts, and
other black communities. They watched the slow, painful
progress of Third World Cinema and other community
production companies to see if they were right.

Lindsay Patterson spoke out against white control of
black films. In a column for the *New York Times* entitled,
"In Movies, Whitey is Still King," he criticized movies
projecting a bad image. "I was never aware before that

so many Hollywood films used Africa as a locale," he said. "Despite the great political, social, and economic changes occurring within the last two decades, the films (and all seem to have been made in the fifties and sixties) persisted in presenting Africa as the lost dark continent, populated by stupid bloodthirsty savages.

"*Beyond Mombasa,* perhaps the worst movie ever made, depicted in one scene, as anthropologically accurate, the most distorted and grotesque caricatures of African tribesmen ever drawn. A more recent film, *The Naked Prey,* offered an excellent study of whitey as supreme. How one unarmed man (Cornel Wilde) could outwit for countless days, on their own terrain, the warriors of an African tribe remains steadfastly beyond my comprehension. But then none of the films attempted to deal with the African as a complex human with a complex culture."

Patterson's point was well taken. Besides an endless series, over three decades, of Tarzan films featuring Elmo Lincoln, Johnny Weissmuller, Jock Mahoney, Buster Crabbe, Gordon Scott, Mike Henry, Lex Barker, Denny Miller, and Ron Ely, there had been a large number of African movies, among which were: *Africa Screams* (1949); *King Solomon's Mines* (1950); *The African Queen* (1952); *Bwana Devil* (1953); *Mogambo* (1953); *White Witch Doctor* (1953); *Tanganyika* (1954); *Hatari!* (1962); *Snows of Kilimanjaro* (1960); *Drums of Africa* (1963); *Call Me Bwana* (1963); *Zulu* (1964); *Rhino* (1964); *Duel in the Jungle* (1965); *Sands of the Kalahari* (1965); *Born Free* (1966); and *Africa—Texas Style* (1967).

Of the 330 films that grossed more than $100,000 in 1970, 14 were black-oriented. (By black-oriented, we

mean films about blacks in American society with at least
one black in a starring or featured role.) Two of the fourteen were declared among the year's ten worst by *New
York* film critic Judith Crist. One was *Last of the Mobile
Hot Shots,* starring Robert Hooks. It was another example
of southern black-white conflict over a white woman and
other problems. The protagonists were half-brothers in
the adaptation of Tennessee Williams's play, *The Seven
Descendants of Myrtle.* The script was improbable and
the film too contrived.

The second was a satire with racial overtones that
brought Pearl Bailey to the screen after almost ten years.
It was called *The Landlord,* and although Judith Crist was
unimpressed, other critics praised it. It was about a rich
young white man who takes ownership of a ghetto tenement in New York and becomes involved with several
black tenants in more than a business relationship. At best
a poor effort.

Jim Brown returned in *tick tick tick,* the story of a
black sheriff in a racially tense southern town. *Tick tick
tick* was more relevant to black audiences than his previous films, and his acting had improved. Brown was also
seen during the year in *The Grasshopper* and *El Condor.*

Racial tension in an American high school was the
theme of *Halls of Anger.* Calvin Lockhart and Janet Mac-
Lachlan starred in this film (which reflected nation-wide
educational turmoil) about the effects of busing white
students to an all-black high school.

Woodstock became a trend-setter after the unprecedented success of the festival and the movie. The Iseley
Brothers, a soul trio from Teaneck, New Jersey, filmed
one of their concerts at the Yankee Stadium. It opened

as *It's Your Thing,* also the title of one of their popular re-cordings. A year later, Cinerama produced *Soul to Soul,* a film account of the marathon jazz-rock festival celebrating Ghana's fourteenth anniversary. It featured Wilson Pick-ett, Ike and Tina Turner, the Staple Singers, Les McCann, and others.

In August, Plaza Pictures released a three-year-old Italian-made Sig Shore film called *Black Jesus,* starring Woody Strode. It was an updated version of the story of Christ, showing the struggle of a black African revolution-ary who is betrayed by a modern Judas. Often effective, this three-year-old revival capitalized on the black boom in movies.

On September 14, radio station WWRL broadcast an ad for a new black-oriented film. The following day the *Daily News* and *New York Post* also ran ads, but without the film's title. "Due to the subject matter . . . for title tune to WLIP radio—1190 or WWRL radio—1600," read a line in the newspaper ads. The film was called *High Yellow* and was about the trials of a light-complexioned black woman. "She didn't cross the color line. She walked right down the middle!" the ads said, but this exploitation film was ignored by reviewers as not worthy of comment. And there were others. Within the next few months, *Honkey, Soul Soldier* (alias *The Red, White and Black*), *Ghetto Freaks,* and even a major studio release, M-G-M's *Cool Breeze,* invaded theaters. Sexploitation film companies like Derio Productions also got into the act, with pictures like *A Place Called Today.*

ABC televised a Screen Gems production called "Brian's Song" in 1971, which featured Billie Dee Williams in the role of Chicago Bears halfback Gayle Sayers. It was the true story of Sayers's friendship with teammate Brian Piccolo (James Caan), who died a tragic early death. After an enthusiastic reception (the film won eleven honors including an Emmy), it was tested in Chicago theaters as a possible feature.

James Earl Jones had followed *The Great White Hope* with a starring role in *The Man,* another ABC Circle Film for television based on a best-selling novel, this about a black man who becomes President of the United States. (Coincidentally, during the month of May, when filming was in progress in the nation's capital, Chicago was unwittingly playing host to prominent blacks who were also discussing what must have been white America's most frightening nightmare—a black presidential candidate. And they were for real.)

Paramount brought *The Man* to theaters and made plans for future showings on television. The performance by James Earl Jones added interest to an otherwise average film. His role was oddly dull, docile, and racially unconscious.

Sparked by the publication of *The Black West, The Buffalo Soldiers in the Indian Wars,* and *The Adventures of the Negro Cowboys,* 1971 and 1972 movies reflected the growing interest of black filmmakers in the role of the black man in the old West.

Woody Strode had appeared in *Sergeant Rutledge* in 1960, and Jim Brown, Ossie Davis, and Sidney Poitier had starred in other westerns of the sixties. There had also been pictures about interior problems, like *The McMasters* with Brock Peters in 1970 and *Soul Soldier* in 1971.

Skin Game, a racial farce starring Lou Gossett, opened late in September. It was the story of a pre-Civil War con

Motown supersongstress Diana Ross in *Lady Sings the Blues*. (Paramount)

Maya Angelou, who wrote both screenplay and score for the motion picture *Georgia, Georgia*. (Kelly-Jordan)

Horace Jackson, left, and Wendell James Franklin, right, were producer and director respectively of *The Bus Is Coming*. (K-Calb)

Jim Brown and Marlene Clark in *Slaughter*. (American Intl.)

Raymond St. Jacques and Godfrey Cambridge put the collar on Tim Pelt in a scene from *Come Back Charleston Blue*. (Warner Bros.)

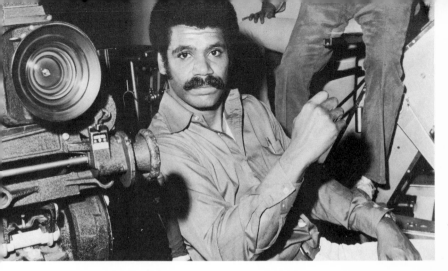

Bill Crain, who directed *Blacula*. (American Intl.)

Scene from *Trouble Man* starring Robert Hooks. (20th Century-Fox)

Buck and the Preacher, starring Harry Belafonte, marked the directorial debut of Sidney Poitier. He also played a co-starring role. (Columbia)

Rupert Crosse and Steve McQueen on *The Reivers* set.

Actor William Marshall in *Blacula,* the first horror film with blacks in all the major roles. (American Intl.)

The family from *Sounder.* (20th Century-Fox)

Lonne Elder, who won an Academy Award nomination for his adaptation of the book *Sounder*. (20th Century-Fox)

The black church is represented in this scene from *Ganja and Hess*. (Kelly-Jordan)

One of the more controversial scenes in the film *Super Fly*. (Warner Bros.)

Bill Gunn, writer and director of *Ganja and Hess.* (Cinerama Releasing)

Diana Sands in *Georgia, Georgia.* (Cinerama Releasing)

Fred Williamson, known as "The Hammer" when he played for the Kansas City football Chiefs. (Paramount)

Film producer and Stax Records vice-president Larry Shaw. (Columbia)

The Limit, directed and produced by and featuring Yaphet Kotto. (Cannon Films)

Ossie Davis spending time with members of his cast in *Black Girl*. (Cinerama Releasing)

man (Jim Garner) who teamed with a slave (Gossett) in a fraudulent sale scheme. After the con man sold the slave—actually a free man born in New Jersey—and collected the money, both disappeared to pull the same trick in another town. The film was perhaps innocently conceived, but it was often offensive and annoying, and probably amused only those who could find humor in the thought of slavery.

John Wayne, a veteran of forty-one years of films, among which were numerous western roles, including a 1970 Oscar-winning performance in *True Grit*, talked to *Playboy* in an interview published in May 1971. Asked if he limited the number of blacks in his pictures, Wayne replied, "Oh, Christ, no. I've directed two pictures and I gave blacks their proper position. I had a slave in *The Alamo* and I had the correct number of blacks in *The Green Berets*. If it's supposed to be a black character, naturally I use a black actor. But I don't go so far as hunting positions for them. I think the Hollywood studios are carrying tokenism too far. There's no doubt that ten percent of the population is black, or colored, or whatever they want to call themselves: they certainly aren't Caucasian. Anyway, I suppose there should be the same percentage of the colored race in films as society. But it can't always be that way. There isn't necessarily going to be ten percent of the grips or sound men who are black because more than likely, ten percent haven't trained themselves for that type of work."

That month, Wayne was on location in New Mexico shooting a western called *The Cowboys*. Wayne had sought the participation of ten major black actors before Roscoe Lee Browne eventually took a role in the film. The

Sanford Production told the story of Wayne leading
eleven youths across the western plains on a cattle drive
in the 1870s. It opened the 1972 season at Radio City
Music Hall, but when the box office began to sag in Chicago six weeks later, revised advertising copy (which had
previously included Wayne's picture only) included a
large picture of Browne and copy that read "also starring
Roscoe Lee Browne as big Duke's valiant sidekick on the
cattle drive."

In October 1971 Sidney Poitier took a print of *Buck
and the Preacher* to Virginia Union University in Richmond, where he showed it at a benefit to raise money to
rebuild a chapel that had burned down. It was homecom-
ing weekend at the Baptist school, and the actor (who is
a member of the Board of Directors) crowned the queen
during halftime on a rainy football afternoon.

Bill Cosby was also on hand that evening, and in typical story-telling form. Cosby had re-edited his western
drama, *Man and Boy,* and had taken out a full page
Variety ad to herald its opening, scheduled for the
Thanksgiving weekend.

Early in December, Utopia Productions announced that
it was readying for distribution a film called *Black Rodeo.*
Six months later Cinerama released the documentary of
a rodeo at New York City's Randall's Island. The film had
black stars and was narrated by Woody Strode.

While Poitier and Cosby were in Richmond, a feature
called *The Legend of Nigger Charley* was in production
elsewhere in Virginia. Former pro footballer Fred Williamson played the title role of a former slave fleeing
white pursuers and trying to make a new start in the
Southwest. For the investment, the picture paid off well,

and as with *Buck and the Preacher,* there was a sequel within a year.

Reading headlines is not the only way the Paris businessman, the Manila student, and the Buenos Aires housewife learn about American society. An effective image-making U. S. export is the motion picture. There is competition from U. S. Information Agency "good guy" classics, but most studios take their foreign distribution seriously, especially since the market for American movies abroad is unpredictable. Even at home U. S. films must meet the formidable challenge of foreign films. With rivals like Clint Eastwood's Italian-made westerns, French romances, and well-made films from increasingly communicative Iron Curtain countries like Czechoslovakia, Hollywood has its work cut out to stay in the race.

Black filmmakers like Ossie Davis are aware of the world-wide black movie market. The European success of Melvin Van Peebles's *The Story of a Three Day Pass* was encouraging, but many black filmmakers believe the largest potential audiences are the African countries.

Plans are being made for a massive cross-oceanic exchange. Black entertainers like Percy Sledge, Wilson Pickett, Eartha Kitt, and James Brown have entertained in Africa. Aretha Franklin even announced plans for what promised to be a controversial concert tour for black audiences in apartheid South Africa. African entertainers like Miriam Makeba, Olatunji, and several dance troupes have become favorites in the U.S.

The universality of blackness in Europe and North and South America and the common tie with Africa is called Pan-Africanism. One weekend late in September 1970, in the complex of Atlanta University, thousands of black

Americans met with African leaders to discuss blackness. One organization represented was the Southern Christian Leadership Conference, the organization of the late Martin Luther King, Jr. Discussion touched on economic and political as well as cultural matters. It was generally agreed that communication should be dramatically increased.

Films can and will be part of that communication, along with interpersonal contact, the ideal (though not always possible) method. African students have been attending American universities for decades, and now more American blacks are vacationing in Black Africa. But the majority of black people will never be fortunate enough to cross oceans and compare cultures. Movies will be their trip.

The exchange is moving into high gear. African filmmakers like Wole Soyinka have come to America and learned necessary techniques. Since the success of Ossie Davis's *Kongi's Harvest* in Nigeria, many black filmmakers are turning east to set up film projects in Africa.

Documentaries about Africa have been made for years. Bill Alexander, who made *Fight Never* and *Souls of Sin* in the United States in the forties, went to London to make films for African governments.

Sidney Poitier appeared in three films in the fifties that dealt with African themes: *Cry, the Beloved Country, Something of Value,* and *Mark of the Hawk.*

In 1972 Poitier and Harry Belafonte made a trip to the African nations of Tanzania and Zambia, by invitation from the presidents of the two countries, to screen *Buck and the Preacher.*

Another African-produced feature that aspired to international audiences was *Bullfrog in the Sun,* a probe of neocolonialism and its consequence—Africa's version of the angry young man. The film's language was English; its money, Black American; its director, German; its screenwriter, Californian; its story, stars, and fabric, African. Among the Nigerian members of the cast was seventy-one-year-old Olando Martin who recalled having made *Hasty Hearts* in 1949 with Ronald Reagan. German filmmaker Jason Pohland's crew was seventy-five percent Nigerian.

Thanksgiving of 1971 had been set for the debut of *Tokoloshe*. It was the story of a young Bantu boy, believed bewitched by an evil spirit, who is forced to leave his primitive homeland and make a journey to Johannesburg, where he enters into a close relationship with a blind man. The film was produced on location in South Africa and brought to America to be screened for reviewers, but did not attract American investors or distributors, probably due to its inability to compete with the more sensational American-made films.

While American blacks were making films in Africa, taking advantage of the facilities offered by the host nations and employing and teaching Africans in the process, an entirely different kind of movie making was taking place in the United States. The basic theme of these pictures centered around conflict between blacks and organized crime, with little attempt at character development or plot. One of the first of these was *Shaft*, in which Richard Roundtree plays a black private detective working out of a Times Square office. The director of the film has his hero walk a delicate line between criminality and law enforcement. His ambiguity allows him to touch upon all those elements that would titillate an audience, but he doesn't linger on any long enough to form an allegiance or indicate personality. He has a black girlfriend but spends one night with a white girl whom he verbally abuses afterwards. He has friends on the police force and among the underworld. In one scene he calls a Mafioso "wop" but only after he has been called a 'nigger.' Eventually he wipes out an entire squad of organized crime members.

Ironically, when *Shaft* was ready for screening, a black man had just shot and critically wounded Joseph Columbo, a man reputedly connected with the same organization that Shaft defeated in the movie. Opening night at the DeMille Theater found nearly as many police in attendance as blacks coming to see the film.

Beginning in 1970 with *Cotton Comes to Harlem,* virtually every black-oriented cops-and-robbers motion picture for three years (with the exception of *Cool Breeze*) dealt in some way with the Mafia. The Mafia were the villains and always took a pronounced image-whipping. And although concerned representatives of the Italian community compelled the producers of *The Godfather* to prohibit use of the word "Mafia," the syndicate and its name were undisguised in *Shaft.* Apparently *Shaft* was not considered important enough to raise concern.

In *Cotton Comes to Harlem* Godfrey Cambridge and Raymond St. Jacques portrayed two off-beat Harlem detectives searching for a bale of cotton stuffed with money. In the course of the film, they strike a bargain with a Mafia operator in a Harlem cafe and (with some pressure) secure a loan.

The Mafia theme persisted in *Shaft's Big Score* and in

the *Cotton* sequel, *Come Back Charleston Blue,* in which two detectives drive the Mafia out of Harlem.

In New York, United Artists filmed *Across 110th Street,* a story of the Harlem numbers bank and the race between cops and mobsters to reach the black operators. In Dallas, Raymond St. Jacques appeared in *The Book of Numbers.* Although set in the 1930s, the themes again were the numbers racket, black gangsters, and the Mafia. In California, Ivan Dixon's first film, *Trouble Man,* starred Robert Hooks as a man hired to settle a growing rivalry between black and white gambling racketeers. Jim Brown's *Slaughter* was about a black veteran returning home to hunt down the Mafia slayers of his relatives.

Despite this emphasis on black-Mafia conflict in black films, its overall effect appeared negligible. A logical inference from the lack of reaction was that blacks did not take such material seriously within the framework of escapist entertainment.

15

Criticism

The number of black newspapers was decreasing, but new black magazines began to appear with more frequency. Two established Johnson publications, the weekly *Jet* and the monthly *Ebony*, ran film features and analyses in most issues. Often they defended films that white reviewers found inferior. But it is probable that black critics could understand better what black filmmakers were trying to communicate and could more accurately predict the reactions of black audiences.

These magazines and others (like *Sepia*) also published a number of features and personality stories. Many important black artists were helped by repeated exposure in the black press.

It was not long before Hollywood had its own black entertainment newspaper and magazine. In Los Angeles, Soul Publications started a splashy, colorful, now-defunct quarterly magazine, *Soul Illustrated*, and a bi-weekly newspaper, *Soul*.

One of the highlights in the paper was a Hollywood column by Walter Burrell, Jr. Burrell was born in Watts and started at Universal as an apprentice publicity writer. Within five years he was a publicist-columnist and a man who knew his way around Hollywood. His columns were full of information on the professional activities of Hollywood blacks and behind-the-scenes glimpses of the industry that American fans delighted in.

In 1969 Burrell was one of seventeen minority group members of the four-hundred-member Publicists Guild. Fifteen were black. Among them were the former Olympic runner Wilma Rudolph, and Vincent Tubbs, a veteran of twenty years and considered a pioneer in the publicity field. A. S. "Doc" Young, who worked with Sidney Poitier on *The Defiant Ones* in 1958 and was credited with the marketing success of *The Bus Is Coming,* was also among the first to become a publicist.

In its Fall 1971 issue, *Soul Illustrated* devoted five articles to a sensitive area of the entertainment business: "The Whites Behind the Blacks."

The careers of successful motion picture actors and actresses are highly organized affairs. Once a potential star is "discovered" (or somehow breaks into the field and signs a contract), specialists devote their daily working hours to assuring the good fortunes of their new acquisition. Such people may be agents, publicists, acting and singing coaches, personal managers, hair stylists, or clothing designers. They are generally unfamiliar to the public, but are often observed smoothing the way in uneasy interviews, chain-smoking backstage at premieres, blowing kisses at press parties, and making transcontinental telephone calls from plush offices.

One inequity in the Hollywood system that has until now escaped public notice is that most of the career-developers and image-creators in the background are white. This poses a problem for the black artist. The people in career management are professionals and may even be dedicated, but the question must be asked: Would the effect be different if blacks managed black careers? The black artist, particularly one who has had dealings with managers of both races, is best qualified to answer.

In the article "A Broad View," Marcia L. Brown wrote, "Examining the American scene as it exists today, one comes to the conclusion that it is very close to impossible for blacks to make it in the entertainment field without white help, and the reason is simply that blacks must rely on whites to promote, manufacture, and buy their product in order for them to be successful. . . . The highly touted $30 billion black market largely goes into the purchase of white-controlled products with only a few exceptions. As a result, black people in all areas of the entertainment field are subject to manipulation by whites. In many cases, their very success or failure lies in the hands of white agents, promoters, or producers."

Whether to sacrifice white expertise in favor of black inexperience—due to a system that had failed to open its doors—was a dilemma confronting many blacks in professional fields.

In November 1971 Johnson Publications announced that it would launch a monthly entertainment magazine called *Black Stars*. The company had redesigned a former women's monthly called *Tan*, automatically transferring its circulation of 117,000 to the new publication. *Black Stars* was to retain some *Tan* features, but would increase coverage of the lives and careers of black entertainers.

Each of New York's general and special interest publications has at least one resident or contributing film critic, and there are at least sixty full- or part-time critics in the city. The number includes few blacks. Perhaps the leading black critic was Clayton Riley, who had written film and drama criticism for the *Liberator* magazine before he began contributing to the *New York Times* in 1969. In "The Black Critic: Theater and Film," an article for the *Amsterdam News*, Riley wrote, "In truth, there is no black critic in the country who can, by himself, destroy any artist's individual creation or his career. Why, then, the continuing barrage of verbal abuse directed at the critics of black art?

"I would like to see a time come when very sincere, very concerned blacks wrote essays intended to shape opinion instead of controlling it where art and artists are concerned. A time when people would not allow themselves to be herded into theater to witness black events that made money for non-black people. (*Shaft* made money for M-G-M Studios. *Sweetback* pays off to a black producer, Melvin Van Peebles). A time when black critical opinion would not be maligned just because it existed but because it sometimes failed, was wrong or misguided. A time when artists, critics, and audiences of black people respected and trusted one another enough to be allies in an effort to have creativity blossoming and growing in all of our communities in the nation. Black artists see. Black critics describe. Both camps could begin to pay more attention to one another."

"New York. New York. So nice you have to say it twice," goes an old saying.

New York had a better-than-average chance of becoming the black movie capital of the world. Old masters like Oscar Michaux called New York home. The classic *Emperor Jones* was filmed there. And recent years had brought a new generation of stage talent, as well as technicians from a handful of training programs. After a confrontation between filmmaker and the community had sparked interest, a Harlem Cinema Foundation was organized. Its goal was to bring more film production into the community. There were thousands of artists in New York who were interested in making films, and at last there was an alternative to the 3,000-mile trek to the West Coast. And that alternative was in their own back yard.

In 1966 Mayor John Lindsay had initiated a movie coordination organization to clear up red tape and expedite movie production in New York. The results were gratifying. Within five years 200 features were filmed entirely in New York. The first one was Sam Goldwyn, Jr.'s *Come Back Charleston Blue,* which was in production at the same time as *Shaft's Big Score* and *Super Fly* and was followed by *Across 110th Street.* But there had been a precedent for black films in New York. *Shaft, Cotton Comes to Harlem, The Landlord, The Angel Levine* and *Putney Swope* had been made there.

By the fall of 1971 thirty productions had been completed since January in which at least part of the filming was done in New York, including police action films like *The Anderson Tapes, The Gang That Couldn't Shoot Straight, The Hot Rock,* and *The Godfather.* Four 1971 Academy Award nominees were New York productions:

The French Connection, The Hospital, Klute, and *Shaft.*

There were four features before the camera when Paramount canceled plans to film *Last of the Red Hot Lovers* and *Play It Again Sam* and moved them to other cities. The announcement was made only weeks before shooting was due to begin on both Broadway adaptations.

The problem was a deadlock in a contract dispute with Local 52 of IATSE. Columbia, United Artists, Twentieth Century-Fox, and Warner Brothers were carrying on concurrent negotiations, and wages for the films then in production had been set for each film individually.

Within a week, a third movie had been moved to the West Coast—*Fuzz,* a comedy about New York police, planned by United Artists and Filmways. It was a blow to blacks in the industry. Third World Cinema and Clif Frazier's Community Film Workshop Council were turning out qualified apprentices and beginning to place them in unions to work on local productions. Suddenly the East Coast job market had tightened as critically as its West Coast counterpart.

On November 10 at a city hall news conference Mayor Lindsay announced that the studios had reached a settlement with Local 52. During four months of negotiations, movie production in New York had been at a virtual standstill. With New York hard-pressed for funds, the mayor characterized income from the $40 million film industry as "not to be sneezed at."

But as the flight from Hollywood continued, other cities such as San Francisco were being used for location shooting. Things had turned sour in New York.

In Hollywood, the mood of summer 1972 was one of anxiety. Across the country, blacks, including national

leaders like Roy Innis and Rev. Jesse Jackson, were beginning to chafe. Even in an acknowledged black film boom,
the onslaught of negative black images had persisted. Box
office receipts occasionally benefited a few blacks, but
never the black community. Concern and even anger were
also growing toward blacks in the industry who were part
of the wrongdoing and tools of the exploiters. Where was
black awareness in Hollywood?

There are 12,000 actors and actresses in Hollywood.
According to estimates, not more than 150 blacks are
included in the total. Perhaps 25 were employed at any
given time, with a dozen of that number on contract to
television. Then local NAACP head Junius Griffin estimated that, in other creative and technical film jobs, less
than one percent of Los Angeles's half-million blacks
were employed.

Though fifteen black-oriented films were ready for
release or in production, work was still difficult to obtain.
Bernie Casey, a co-star in *Boxcar Bertha,* said, "I suppose
a great many people want to believe that there is a real
deluge of black films coming on but there's not, primarily
because most black actors are still out of work. It's also
important to realize that it's hard to judge the growth of
black films when there had been none."

Unemployed television director Luther James sat on
the terrace of a Sunset Boulevard cafe and mused, "These
black films don't represent any basic change in business
à la Hollywood. They are black staffed, but that's all.
Black people take part on an employee basis and don't
have liberty to work freely. It's tokenism straight up and
down."

Stories circulated about black directors—often teamed with white producers—being pressured to accelerate already abbreviated production schedules. On location at three such films, new directors and producers were at odds with studio busybodies and unit production "supervisors." The opposition formerly confronting only performers now struck at another group. Directors who had overcome odds and found work had to battle the studios for artistic control.

In the Twentieth Century-Fox commissary (after completing the shooting of *Trouble Man* with director Ivan Dixon), Robert Hooks described the attitude at the studios:

"I think the most important factor is that white people still have not grown out of the god complex of thinking that they really know us. And they don't. They would like to think they are authorities on what's black, but it's been proven not so. I'm totally convinced, after doing *Trouble Man*, that my producers don't know black people—and that's basically the problem."

Fred Williamson (known as "The Hammer" during his one-year career with the Kansas City football Chiefs) had been working more often than other actors. His controversially titled film, *The Legend of Nigger Charley*, had earned more than the original investment. Another film, *Hammer*, was awaiting release, and he had begun work on a western sequel to *Charley*.

Referring to the new demand for black films, he said, "It's definitely created more jobs because you've got more black people doing more work, but the people doing these movies are still unhappy to the extent that black movies are not really a depiction of what they really want them

158 *To Find an Image*

to be. We do the work because we need the bread, and it gives us the power to do the things that we want to do.

"*Nigger Charley* was a good movie, but there were things about it that were purely commercialized for the sake of making money. It's a dog-eat-dog business, black and white. They are exploiting the hell out of us, but while they are exploiting us, they are giving us power. Once you get a track record, you can go out and demand things."

Actress Gwen Mitchell discussed the way hero figures, like those in *Nigger Charley* and *Shaft* (in which she co-starred), affected black actresses. She felt strongly that there was very little opportunity for black actresses, primarily because there were so few decent parts for black males. She was not being given the chance to play non-racial roles, nor did she particularly care to play in exploitation movies.

"I do feel that the black actress has to write scripts for herself, and that's what I've started to do. The only way you're going to get a true black female image on screen—and that's what I'm concerned about—is by writing it yourself. And I don't think that's too farfetched."

Most of those interviewed believed markets for the bad films would dry up. While blacks were encouraged by the prediction, it was not welcomed by investors, who were earning large yearly profits on an estimated $110 million from black moviegoers.

"I feel that the black films that are being accepted today are being produced just for commercial value," Miss Mitchell said. "A year or two from now, people are not going to want to touch them. They're going to say no. We want something valid. We want to see some truth."

An actor, Bernie McCain, said the industry "made only three or four good films a year as opposed to four hundred failures. They've been making films since D. W. Griffith, and we have for two years, and yet we feel we've got to come out heavy every time. For every black film made, there are people learning their craft. There are black actors working. There is a black director, hopefully, or maybe a black cinematographer or editor or a black man to score it.

"We know they will still be white films until we are producing them, making them, financing them, and reaping the reward. Until we get to that point, you're going to have films that aren't together."

But the alternative—independent production—was building momentum.

"Black picturemakers are here to stay," Horace Jackson, of K-Calb, was convinced. "It's going to take zeal for us to get through," he said of blacks who chose the independent route. "We have to do first things first, and that means finding capital for blacks. Black banks have been intimidated by the mention of losses, and they feel that anything that has to do with film has a loss built in."

First-time director Raymond St. Jacques, who completed *Book of Numbers* with funds supplied by Brut Productions, complained that black investors were "conservative," and that he had been forced to seek out white financing.

Ironically, the new black films were proving to be blue-chip investments. Even with an unprecedented average of four a month (totaling over fifty since 1970), nearly all were clearing the first hurdle—breaking even—and earning some profit besides.

Singer-composer Jerry Butler, an aspiring black producer, said, "I think that if black films are going to be done and be meaningful to black people in a real sense, they're going to have to be financed by black dollars. Otherwise, we're going to wind up producing the type of films that the folks with the dollars will allow us to produce."

Only one black company was in a position to finance its first film without outside help. Motown's *Lady Sings the Blues* was to open in October. When the music conglomorate moved west from Detroit that summer, it had also shifted creative emphasis to a new area. President Berry Gordy, Jr. took a personal interest in his first film project. When disagreements with the studio developed, he bought out other investors in order to retain artistic control of the movie. New York-based Melvin Van Peebles, a controversial figure in black Hollywood, remained the only black producer-director to have worked in Hollywood and broken away—totally and successfully.

The sprawling geography of southern California had greatly limited contact between artists in Hollywood's black colony, though they sometimes met at popular private clubs like the Candy Store, the Sports Page, and Bumbles. But summer brought new awareness and togetherness. In June, Wendell Franklin called a meeting of black directors to discuss ways of gaining creative authority. Robert Hooks announced his three-year-old desire to organize Nation Time Productions, a multi-media production company, to be sponsored by black investors and to include leading black entertainers and artists.

During work on *Melinda*, producer Pervis Atkins looked at the sign on his desk at M-G-M: The Buck Stops Here . . . Sometimes. "The impetus for change has to come from the outside, but enough people in the industry are not going to cop out," he said. "Still, we should be looking toward having studios where the principal output would be black and the ownership likewise."

Since the early 1930s, when Hollywood began importing black singers and dancers from New York theaters and nightclubs, there has been a large assemblage of East Coast talent working in the film capital. Hollywood faced a major challenge as black migration and mobilization continued.

One former New Yorker was screenwriter Lonne Elder III (of *Sounder* and *Melinda*), who organized the Sunday afternoon symposium "The Emergence of Black Films: A Blessing or a Curse?" in July. Elder chaired a nine-member panel that analyzed all aspects of the industry for a crowd of 400 listeners at the Los Angeles discotheque, Maverick's Flat.

Emphasis was on "getting together to protect ourselves," and on the need for a strong black film industry. The formation of a Black Artists Alliance during the meeting was a move in that direction.

There would be additional meetings, Elder assured the group. "I would just like to see more of us organizing and coming together—not just to hold symposiums, but to do our thing, to do our work." The alliance began to meet regularly to discuss matters of concern, such as the *Hollywood Reporter's* "racist" review of the film *Sounder*.

The outside support many artists hoped for emerged at the end of summer. For more than three years the Hollywood-Beverly Hills chapter of the NAACP had been generating an awareness of black problems, sparking Justice Department lawsuits to bolster minority membership in trade unions, and focusing on black achievement with the annual Image Awards for outstanding merit in the arts. In an August speech, chapter president Junius Griffin denounced the "super nigger" image in recent black films. Only five years earlier the description had been applied only to parts played by Sidney Poitier. With the rise of other black dramatic stars, the "super nigger" epidemic had grown to "devastating proportions."

The widely publicized speech was significant confirmation of a growing backlash of blacks outside the industry. Something had to be done, Griffin declared. Representatives of local NAACP, CORE, and SCLC chapters had therefore formed a group to rate films according to black standards. The new Coalition Against Blaxploitation had assigned *Black Stars's* critic and columnist Walter Burrell to head CAB's five-member rating committee. Films would be classified as superior, good, acceptable, objectionable, or thoroughly objectionable. Reinforced by film boycotts and grass roots protests, the ratings would spur concessions from the studios.

In condemning the industry's exploitation of black artists, the CAB did not win Hollywood's heart. It was conceded that public recognition of dishonest black film characterizations was imperative. But even blacks had reservations about the CAB ratings as the means to this objective. Black audiences were more likely to be guided by word-of-mouth opinion. And black artists, already battling discrimination, unemployment, and cutthroat competition, would be under added pressure. The system, like the MPAA's code, was a license to limit creative freedom.

A point on which Griffin and the Black Artists Alliance were agreed was the need for Jesse Jackson. As a liaison with blacks across the country, he could explain the problems faced by his brothers and sisters in the film industry.

As artists in Hollywood struggled through a period of transition and uncertainty, Bernie McCain typified advocates of non-intervention:

"We place tremendous restrictions on our creativity in that everything we do has to be a masterpiece. But we simply must be allowed to fail, because out of that comes a certain kind of growth, a certain kind of maturity, a certain kind of awareness and we cannot expect—it's unrealistic to expect or believe—that every film is going to be great."

Anxiety continued to grow. Black actors and actresses were taking closer looks at roles, demanding changes in some and refusing others.

Pointing to the failure of "relevant" black films, and claiming black audiences were getting what they wanted, the industry was nevertheless showing signs of confusion. Some black productions were postponed or canceled, but there was some effort at compromise. When it opened in September, *Sounder,* an Atlanta Film Festival winner from Twentieth Century-Fox, became the first film with a non-sensationalist, human story about blacks. Three films by young black directors—*Super Fly,* by Gordon Parks, Jr., *Top of the Heap,* by Christopher St. John, and *The Limit,* by Yaphet Kotto—were completed independently and brought to studios for distribution. By fall, two respected plays, *Black Girl* and *No Place To Be Somebody,* were in production.

"If a product has a market," Luther James said, "eventually good things will come and drive out the bad. That's if it's an honest game."

A movement to break from the restrictions of Hollywood

was under way. People said it had to happen. And they were all excited; for years they had been saving special projects to do when they had more freedom. They knew there was a market for new ideas, and they pledged that today's artistic slaves would be tomorrow's liberators.

It was time for the late news in New York City. In a small television studio on West 53rd Street on November 9, 1971, an audience was gathered for a Channel Thirteen program produced by three young women. The ninety-minute show was "Free Time," and Ossie Davis, Gordon Parks, and Melvin Van Peebles were booked, for the first time since finishing their latest films, for a public discussion of black filmmaking.

Air time was eleven o'clock. The principals took their places on the set. Gordon Parks walked out first, searching the crowd of eighty for familiar faces. He was wearing an expensive suit and a turtleneck shirt. Melvin Van Peebles was next, in jeans, suede boots, a black turtleneck, and a gray jacket. Parks crossed his legs; Van Peebles slouched in his chair. Ossie Davis took his place, smiling and waving at film students in the crowd. He was dressed casually in slacks and sport shirt.

A question was directed at the first two panelists. Why had Davis (in *Cotton Comes to Harlem*) and Parks (in *Shaft*) shown policemen as hero figures?

"*Cotton* was a job offered me," Davis replied, "my first opportunity to direct a film. Chester Himes wrote the original story and the two characters were cops. It was more a case of the material choosing me than me choosing the material."

"I did *Shaft* because I thought it was a fun film," Parks

said. John Shaft was a private detective, he pointed out, not a cop. "It gave me relief from some of the serious problems I faced every day."

Van Peebles had been waiting for the second question. Should black films be political?

"Definitely," he answered. "Black films should deal with images of our position in the superstructure. They should all work toward the decolonization of black minds and the reclaiming of black spirit."

"All films are political," Davis added. "If I had total control, I would choose to be political. My relationship to politics, however, is a little more subtle. I place my emphasis on behind-the-scene politics. I try to get money that's taken from the community back into the community."

Parks had another approach, explaining, "I paid my dues and that's political. I've opened a lot of doors. This is what I call power. M-G-M gave in to my requests and so did Warner Brothers."

Julius Lester questioned whether the "political thing" was too narrow a path to follow.

Van Peebles took the initiative. "I bring along other technicians with other points of view. My role is the training of technicians in order to break through economic boundaries."

Lester asked about the problems of working in Hollywood. Davis summed up, "The choice of materials and employees is determined by those who have no direct knowledge of the black experience."

The most fascinating replies came from the three directors when they were asked what film they would make if they had complete freedom.

Davis stated that if he "had all the money I needed and a top-flight black crew," he would do an adaptation of Alex Haley's study of blacks from America back to their roots in Africa. Van Peebles said he would direct a comedy, *Don't Play Us Cheap*, then a return of Sweetback, a western, and finally a second return of Sweetback.

Parks wanted to direct a "great dramatization" of the black revolt. It would probably be his most significant film, he added, although 1971 was too early to begin.

16

About Money

Shaft was leading with a gross estimated by director Gordon Parks at $18 million. His son Gordon, Jr.'s first effort, *Super Fly*, quickly caught up with *Shaft*.

Every week, *Variety* publishes the cumulative grosses (money taken in at box offices) of the top fifty American films currently running. The figures do not indicate net profits, but they are barometers of public taste. Net gross is determined by computing attendance reports from exhibitors. The leaking of inflated figures (a practice of distributors and producers) makes an accurate tally difficult.

Deducted from the gross are a host of costs, including theater owners' percentages, promotion, and publicity. These "below-the-line" costs are a sample of the 237 types of accounts or expenses compiled by one studio as a guide for film-producing companies.

In the same category are production costs—camera rental, film, material to build sets, props, and salaries for the crew. Technical and support crews are union members paid according to a graduated scale.

"Above-the-line" costs are the cast, the directors, and

the producer's unit. Also under this heading were story rights and continuity. If the screenplay is based on a novel, story, or play, a fee must be paid for rights to the material.

When these costs have been subtracted, the profit is often a small percentage of the film's gross receipts. But who gets the money when there is a profit?

There are some 14,000 motion picture theaters in the country. Blacks own less than twenty; none in New York City. And it is theater owners who earn substantial sums when films are successful.

When a movie is bringing in business, the theater is automatically reimbursed for the "house nut," or weekly operating expenses. In New York City's first-run theaters, operating costs range from $4,800 a week (at the tiny Cinema II) to $16,500 (at the mammoth Rivoli, Loew's State I and II, and the Ziegfeld). Expenses include rent, salaries, insurance, and taxes. When they are cleared, the remaining box office receipts are divided between theater owner and distributor on a percentage basis.

There are weeks when theaters don't take in enough for the house nut. So when a film clears the nut in *one day* (as *Super Fly* did at the Loew's State II in August 1972), it's a runaway success. By fall 1972 black films were being held over with mounting enthusiasm by theater owners impressed by the profits if not the performances.

For their effort in the filmmaking process, some producers and distributors feel that theater owners—the only men enjoying direct contact with the consumer and his dollars—are succeeding magnificently. Black artists, on the other hand, are faring relatively poorly. The majority of Hollywood's black-oriented movies are produced by whites for a single purpose—to exploit a lucrative new market.

These inferior films, however, will one day be examined critically as part of "black" cinema. By "discovering" unknown actors, producers can keep salaries at the minimum level. Nearly every black movie has a new star whose name no one has heard before and will probably never hear again, while established black actors and actresses go without work. The forty or so black artists who are regularly employed average between $20,000 and $60,000 a year.

Except for the black superstar. Sidney Poitier can still command a $1 million fee, twice the salary of any other black actor or actress. Closest to Poitier in earnings is Jim Brown, who was paid $37,000 in 1963 to do a film (*Rio Conchos*) between football seasons. By 1969 Brown's going rate (for 100 *Rifles*) was $200,000 and five percent of the net.

Although Diana Sands (*Georgia, Georgia*), Cicely Tyson (*Sounder*), and Diana Ross (*Lady Sings the Blues*) were considered for Oscars, no black actress since Dorothy Dandridge has shown the box office power of Poitier and Brown for long enough to approach the salary level of the two superstars.

Black actors and actresses have never had financial parity with their white counterparts, partly because black films were thought a gamble. Many in the industry were undoubedly convinced of the hazards after Twentieth Century-Fox made a film version of the Broadway hit, *The Great White Hope,* investing $10 million in the project. When *Hope* was released in 1970 it was a box office bomb, grossing only $600,000 by the end of the year.

Moreover, as if justifying low-budget productions, two independent, virtually non-union films, each made for less than $500,000, turned the industry upside down. *Sweet Sweetback* and *Super Fly* captured black audiences with their nitty-gritty approach and their use of the ghetto and its language. Each film grossed over $10 million within three months of release. The industry may have ignored the creative reasons for the success stories, but they did not forget the costs; two quality feature films had been done on budgets major studios would have allotted for better cartoons and short subjects. When *Blacula, Melinda,* and *Trouble Man* were in production in the summer of 1972, there were plans to tighten tight budgets and shorten short production schedules.

With the handful of independent features included, the average cost of black-oriented films produced since 1970 was $700,000. The overall Hollywood average exceeds $1 million. The musical *Sweet Charity*, for instance, was made for $8 million.

Perhaps the most publicized example of this was the reported $13,500 that *Shaft* star Richard Roundtree, a newcomer, was paid for his work. Even with the financial success of the second *Shaft* film (in which he fought unsuccessfully for a $50,000 salary), Roundtree's scale has not matched his box office power.

A film actor's income depends on how often he works and on the importance of each role. Press agents casually name the amounts paid white film stars and quote fantastic sums spent on Hollywood epics. The era of the epic is gone, but outsiders still imagine such excesses. When newcomers to moviemaking arrive, they bring their big budget concepts with them. Motown Records announced *Lady Sings the Blues* as its first major undertaking and

was the only black corporation in the entertainment world
that could make such an investment.

At first $5 million (one-third of Motown's total film
budget) was set aside for the musical biography. But
shooting was confined to California, and the final cost—
just over $3 million—still made *Lady* the most expensive
black production of the seventies.

The independent black producer has found raising capital outside Hollywood nearly impossible. The list of starts
and corresponding failures is long. Recently Ivan Dixon
and Sam Greenlee attempted to produce a film version of
Greenlee's novel, *The Spook Who Sat by the Door*. The
production, budgeted at about $800,000, died just as
filming in Gary, Indiana was set to begin. (But the film
was later completed—under budget—on the West Coast.)
Ossie Davis's Third World Cinema in New York failed
after two years of effort to get a film into production, even
though a distribution agreement (with Twentieth Century-Fox) for its first five films had already been signed.

Actor Raymond St. Jacques was forced to sign with Brut
Productions, a subsidiary of Fabergé, to finance his *Book
of Numbers*, budgeted at $700,000. He complained of re-
buffs from potential black investors, and his anger was
typical of a growing resentment among black artists. They
found inexplicable the stubborn refusals of wealthy blacks
who reneged despite the overwhelming success of black
films.

Perhaps it was the difficulty of collecting the profits that
continued to frighten off black film backers. St. Jacques
admitted it had been two years since the filming of *Cotton
Comes to Harlem* before his first residual payments had
come in. The neophyte independent K-Calb Productions,

which finished *The Bus Is Coming* despite overwhelming odds, watched the film gross $4 million in its first six months, but president Horace Jackson was forced to threaten legal action to recover his fair share from the distributor.

In the summer of 1972 there was a backlash against the flood of new black films. The argument entered a new stage. It was not only negative images that outraged the black community; films had been degrading blacks for decades. As spokesmen outside the industry jockeyed for position and authority to negotiate with the studios, it was clear that certain groups were looking for a piece of the action.

It started in May 1972 when CORE's Roy Innis announced the formation of a Harlem Cinema Foundation to encourage movie production in the black community. In return filmmakers would have to agree to several conditions, including employment of more blacks on black-oriented films, payment to black banks of a share of the profits, and endowment of a fund for the training of apprentices.

The announcement came when the cast and crew of *Come Back Charleston Blue* were ordered out of Harlem following a "misunderstanding," and denied permission to return even after a series of negotiations. At Innis's press conference, the community's gamble in demanding a percentage of a film's profit was pointed out. Suppose the films did not make a profit?

Despite pledges of cooperation from several filmmakers, nothing more was heard of the foundation. No black films came to New York for at least four months, according to Mayor Lindsay's film coordinator. Innis's new-found interest in a film industry had not been dampened. He was quoted in praise of the depression family tale, *Sounder*. On NBC-TV's "Today Show," he debated star Ron O'Neal over the merits of the drug drama *Super Fly* which, ironically, had been allowed total freedom to film in Harlem. He showed up in Hollywood in the midst of industry backlash and announced that CORE was planning a film of its own. With amazing aplomb Innis revealed that he would solicit a $3 million investment from Warner Brothers, the company he had criticized for distributing *Super Fly*.

Dissidents claim a moral right to demand funds from the industry, based on the large percentage of blacks regularly attending downtown theaters—usually paying two to four dollars and usually willing to stand in line to see black films. What most activists want is a return from the money spent by blacks to enrich the industry. Assuming an amount equal to the "entertainment" received is deducted, it is unclear how much activists feel is due the community. A popular solution would be the donation of sufficient funds to develop a separate black film industry chiefly through the training of behind-the-camera personnel. The goal is commendable, but negotiators have not agreed on the mechanics of the plan.

The future is hopeful. With independent producers and production companies taking up the slack, a turnabout in domestic filmmaking has arrived. And as reported in *Variety* in July, the 1972 box office in key cities was up twenty-three percent, or $36 million, over 1971.

As of October 1972 grosses for five top black films were estimated as: *Super Fly*—$11 million; *Shaft's Big Score*—$10 million; *Buck and the Preacher*—$9 million; and *The*

Legend of Nigger Charley and *Melinda*—$5 million apiece. The total: $40 million. And the figures did not include twenty-two black films which by then had been released, some of which (*Blacula, Slaughter, Sounder,* and *Lady Sings the Blues*) were drawing enthusiastic crowds. The totals and their impact on the movie industry speak for themselves.

It was the chance for money, not good films, that made Hollywood the movie capital of the world. It was the loss of money that challenged Hollywood's status. It was partly the promise of money that brought over fifty black actors, actresses, directors, and writers from the New York stage to the West Coast film center over the past fifteen years. And it was money that recently brought a number of blacks to Hollywood, at first blowing clouds of angry smoke but eventually imitating the white exploiters.

The dollar is the overriding consideration in making a feature film, especially today. When a winning formula like *Shaft* appeared, Hollywood was willing to allow black directors relative freedom as long as profits continued. The more profit, the more latitude. Judging from offers Melvin Van Peebles received after *Sweetback,* he might have been permitted to make such a "revolutionary" film for Hollywood if studios had been convinced it would bring in as much money as *Sweetback.*

People have a need to be entertained, and movies are the largest source of out-of-the-home entertainment for blacks, long starved for images of themselves. For many a black man, there was hypnotic fascination in the sight of himself on screen and in identifying with events in a film.

And there was curiosity. Black people who knew by

talking to friends that they would not like a certain movie stood in long lines and paid to see it anyway because it was black-oriented. Over the protests of idealists in the black community, the greatest response was to those standard favorites, the action feature and the western. Audience identification was keyed to black film stars, who quickly become a primary factor in film selection. Weekend moviegoing was already traditional with some blacks. The question was whether they would see an exploitative film or a relevant one.

The audience at a black-oriented movie is a unique spectacle. The raucous cheers and jeers from *Uptight* to *Sweetback* left theatergoers with ringing ears, wondering if they had been to a movie or a football game. Black heroes were winning, and the soul slaps and knowing smiles of satisfied audiences were evidence that blacks wanted films made especially for them. Whatever their quality, black films had a market.

17

The Future of
Black Cinema

The first problem of black cinema is survival. When a new black women's magazine appeared several years ago, it was very distinctive due to the picture of a lovely black girl on the cover. The following month there were two other magazines on the stands with cover portraits of black women. By the time of its second issue the new magazine was being challenged.

Black filmmakers are being challenged by white producers and studios who see in the black film a source of easy revenue. The films that the studios employ blacks to produce and direct are no different from exploitation films made by whites. To say that the answer lies with black investors would be to oversimplify. People with enough money to produce a film must be found. These people must choose film investments rather than securities or futures or other proven financial ventures. After a film is produced it must be profitably distributed. Mishandling at any point can completely wipe out profits.

Film producers support distributors who support

theater owners, and the process also works in reverse. Each element of the industry supports the others. Independent film producers are forced to buck the whole system. Books from independent black publishers have been refused by bookstores and ignored by critics. Black film producers face the same problem. The future of independent black film companies is therefore uncertain despite the success of Van Peebles or some of the early black filmmakers. Even now, as a major black talents emerge, they are largely absorbed into white production companies. It is probable, then, that black films will be an influence and a force within the American cinema rather than a separate entity.

That is not to say there will be no independent black filmmakers. There have been black companies for over fifty years, and some undoubtedly will continue to flourish. But there are already indications that independent companies will not play the largest part in bringing black images to the screen. The companies springing up on both coasts have not yet shown the capacity for sustained productivity. Much of the impetus for these companies comes from the increased amount of trained black personnel.

Thanks to occasional help from the government and opportunities won for them by Belafonte, Poitier, Greaves, Van Peebles, Davis, and others, hundreds of young blacks have been trained in the scores of jobs required to make a feature film. Some are now working for the major studios. Others are supplying the needs of black producers and black production companies.

In other creative areas, there has been progress. John O. Killins, Ossie Davis, Lorraine Hansberry, William Branch, and Lonne Elder are among the blacks who have written feature films.

Blacks have also begun composing music for films. Three-time Academy Award nominee Quincey Jones scored forty films between 1966 and 1971. The music from *Shaft,* by Isaac Hayes, was a spectacular success and earned a gold record within weeks of its release. It sold as a single and as an album. The recorded sound track eventually earned platinum status, signifying two million dollars in sales. Hayes won several awards, including a Grammy and an Academy Award, for his first effort.

Film editor Hugh A. Robertson has made olympic strides. After winning an Academy Award nomination for his work with *Midnight Cowboy,* he moved on to *Shaft,* became a consultant on *Georgia, Georgia,* and then directed his first feature, *Hang Tough!* for M-G-M.

Greaves and Van Peebles are examples of the growing number of black filmmakers who have proved their cinematic ability and won prestigious film honors.

The black film itself has become the subject of serious study. Black film festivals were held at Knoxville College in 1970, at Spelman and Rutgers in 1971, and at the University of Pennsylvania in 1973. They offered the chance to study the old, compare the present, and talk about the future. With intellectual interest in black films, research and writing on the topic is increasing.

Organizations like the Hollywood chapter of the NAACP, and *Soul* are now giving film awards.

The creation of an image is one of the primary objectives of black filmmakers.

It may take five years. It may take longer, but there will come a day when a black man—any black man in the world—will walk into a theater, see himself in a movie, and learn something while being entertained. Something that will stimulate his emotions and increase his pride and self-respect. Something that will generate his concern for his fellow man. Something that will transform that concern into involvement. Something that will identify and communicate blackness, like an Aretha Franklin concert, a Malcolm X speech, a storefront church service, a Don Lee poem, or a young brother with billowing afro.

An image, a symbol, a style, a heritage. Something any black man will look at and about which he will say, "That's me . . . and it's good."

Black Cinema.

Appendix

THE ESTABLISHMENT

Member Companies—Motion Picture Association of America

Twentieth Century-Fox
Columbia Pictures
United Artists
Paramount Pictures
Universal

Warner Brothers
Metro-Goldwyn-Mayer
Avco Embassy
Allied Artists

Other Major Distributors

National General Pictures
Cinerama Releasing Corporation
Cinema 5
Buena Vista
American International
Universal-Marion
Cannon
Cinemation
Sherpix

V.I. Productions
Commonwealth United
Chevron
Art Films International
Grove Press
Aquarius
Eve Productions
Audubon
Continental

LABOR

Hollywood

Affiliated Prop Craftsmen
American Federation of Television and Radio Artists
American Guild of Variety Artists
Directors Guild of America
Film Technicians (Lab)
IATSE & MPMO
International Brotherhood of Electrical Workers (electricians)
IPMPI (cameramen)
International Sound Technicians
Make-up Artists and Hair Stylists
Motion Picture Costumers
Motion Picture Electricians
Motion Picture Film Editors
Motion Picture Illustrators

Motion Picture Studio Cinetechnicians
Motion Picture Studio Grips
NABET-AFC
Publicists
Screen Actors Guild
Screen Cartoonists
Screen Extras
Script Supervisors
Set Designers and Model Makers
Society of Motion Picture Art Directors
Sound Construction, I & M
Studio Transportation Drivers
Theatrical Stage Employees
Writers Guild West

181

LABOR Continued

New York

American Federation of Musicians
American Guild of Music Arts
Association of Film Craftsmen,
   NABET
Association of Theater Agents
   and Managers
Film Exchange Employees Union
Motion Picture Assistant
   Directors

Motion Picture Lab Technicians
Motion Picture Studio Mechanics
Moving Picture Machine
   Operators
Screen Actors Guild
Treasurers and Ticket Sellers
United Scenic Artists

BLACK FILMS OF 1973

Trick Baby   Universal
Black Mama, White Mama   AIP
Black Caesar   AIP
Wattstax   Columbia
The Harder They Fall   (Independent)
Book of Numbers   Avco Embassy
The Mack   Cinerama
Ganja and Hess   Kelly-Jordan
Let the Good Times Roll   Columbia
A Warm December   NGP
Sweet Jesus Preacher Man   M-G-M
Charley One Eye   Paramount
Coffy   AIP
Shaft in Africa   M-G-M
Super Fly TNT   Paramount
The Soul of Nigger Charley   Paramount
Cleopatra Jones   WB
Gordon's War   Fox
Scream Blacula Scream   AIP
Slaughter's Big Ripoff   AIP
The Spook Who Sat by the Door   UA
Save the Children   Paramount
Maurie   NGP
Savage   New World
Hit   Paramount
The Slams   M-G-M
Jimi Plays Berkeley   (Independent)
Five on the Black Hand Side   UA
Black Bart   WB
Lost in the Stars   (Independent)
Three the Hard Way   AA
The House on Skull Mountain   Columbia
Honey Baby Honey Baby   Kelly-Jordan

BLACK FILMS OF 1972

Soul Soldier   Fanfare
Georgia, Georgia   Cinerama
Man and Boy   Levitt-Pickman
Cool Breeze   M-G-M
Buck and the Preacher   Columbia
The Legend of Nigger Charley   Paramount
Top of the Heap   Fanfare
Malcolm X   WB
Shaft's Big Score   M-G-M
Come Back Charleston Blue   WB
Black Rodeo   Cinerama
The Final Comedown   New World
The Limit   Cannon
Super Fly   WB
The Man   Paramount
Blacula   AIP
Melinda   M-G-M
Sounder   Fox
Hammer   UA
Hickey and Boggs   UA
Lady Sings the Blues   Paramount
Black Girl   Cinerama
Farewell Uncle Tom   Cannon
Trouble Man   Fox
Hit Man   M-G-M
Black Gunn   Columbia
Across 110th Street   UAB

BLACK FILMS OF 1971

The Ali-Frazier Fight
Black Chariot
Black Jesus
Brian's Song
Brother John
The Bus Is Coming
High Yellow
Honkey
Man and Boy
The Man from C.O.T.T.O.N.

The Organization
Right On
Skin Game
Soul Soldier
Soul to Soul
Shaft
Sweet Sweetback's Badasssss
    Song
Uncle Tom's Cabin

BLACK FILMS OF 1970

A.K.A. Cassius Clay
Angel Levine
Cotton Comes to Harlem

Halls of Anger
It's Your Thing
The Landlord

BLACK FILMS OF 1970 Continued

They Call Me Mister Tibbs
The Last of the Mobile Hotshots
The Great White Hope
The Liberation of L. B. Jones

tick tick tick
The McMasters
Watermelon Man

FILMS OF THE SIXTIES

Burn!   1969
Change of Mind   1969
100 Rifles   1969
Putney Swope   1969
The Learning Tree   1969
The Lost Man   1969
Two Gentlemen Sharing   1969

Dark of the Sun   1968
For Love of Ivy   1968
*If He Hollers Let Him
   Go*   1968
Joanna   1968
The Scalphunters   1968
Slaves   1968
Uptight   1968

The Dutchman   1967
*Guess Who's Coming
   to Dinner*   1967
Hurry Sundown   1967
In the Heat of the Night   1967
Portrait of Jason   1967
*The Story of a Three
   Day Pass*   1967
To Sir With Love   1967

The Battle of Algiers   1966
The Girl Nobody Knew   1966

A Patch of Blue   1965

Black Like Me   1964
The Cool World   1964
One Potato, Two Potato   1964
Nothing but a Man   1964

An Affair of the Skin   1963
Gone Are the Days   1963
To Kill a Mockingbird   1963

A Taste of Honey   1962

A Raisin in the Sun   1961
Take a Giant Step   1961
Tomango   1961
The Young One   1961

I Passed for White   1960
All the Young Men   1960
Sergeant Rutledge   1960
Shadows   1960
Walk Like a Dragon   1960

BLACK FILMS OF THE FIFTIES

Anna Lucasta   1959
Black Orpheus   1959
Imitation of Life   1959
Odds Against Tomorrow   1959
Porgy and Bess   1959

The Defiant Ones   1958
The Mark of the Hawk   1958
St. Louis Blues   1958

Something of Value   1957
Island in the Sun   1957

Carmen Jones   1954

Bright Road   1953
The Joe Louis Story   1953

Cry, the Beloved Country   1952

Native Son   1951

The Breaking Point   1950
*The Jackie Robinson
   Story*   1950
No Way Out   1950

BLACK FILMS OF THE FORTIES

Home of the Brave   1949
Lost Boundaries   1949
Pinky   1949
Intruder in the Dust   1949

The Burning Cross   1947
Sepia Cinderella   1947
Ebony Parade   1947
Reet, Petite and Gone   1947
New Orleans   1947
Song of the South   1947
Uncle Tom's Cabana   1947

Angel on My Shoulder   1946
Till the End of Time   1946
Night and Day   1946
The Brotherhood of Man   1946
Beware   1946
The Sailor Takes a Wife   1946
The Man on America's
   Conscience   1946
Smooth as Silk   1946
Mildred Pierce   1946
Hold That Blonde   1946
Memory for Two   1946
The Scarlet Clue   1945
Ziegfeld Follies   1946
Brewster's Millions   1946

We've Come a Long
   Way   1945
Gentle Annie   1945
Jammin' the Blues   1945
Dr. George Washington
   Carver   1945
Negro Colleges in
   Wartime   1945
Bowery to Broadway   1945
Dixie Jamboree   1945
Dark Waters   1945
The House I Live In   1945
The Negro Sailor   1945

The Curse of the
   Cat People   1944
Sahara   1944
Boogie Woogie Dream   1944
The Negro Soldier   1944
Lifeboat   1944
Carnival in Rythmn   1944

Cabin in the Sky   1943
Crime Smasher   1943
Bataan   1943
I Walk with a Zombie   1943
Crash Dive   1943
Strange Incident   1943
Something to Shout
   About   1943
Tales of Manhattan   1943
Casablanca   1943
The Vanishing Virginian   1943
Dixie   1943
Stormy Weather   1943
Gallant Lady   1943

Cairo   1942
The Talk of the Town   1942
Henry Brown, Farmer   1942
In This Our Life   1942
The Body Disappears   1942

Virginia   1941
Affectionately Yours   1941
Birth of the Blues   1941
Lucky Ghost   1941
Sunday Sinners   1941
A Place to Live   1941
Murder on Lenox
   Avenue   1941
King of the Zombies   1941
Maryland   1941
Keep Punching   1941

The Ghost Breakers   1940
One Tenth of Our
   Nation   1940
Chasing Trouble   1940
Golden Boy   1940
Swanee River   1940
Broken Strings   1940
Mr. Washington Goes
   to Town   1940

BLACK FILMS OF THE THIRTIES

Gone with the Wind   1939
Young Mr. Lincoln   1939
Man About Town   1939
Way Down South   1939
Harlem on the Prairie   1939
*The Adventures of
  Huckleberry Finn*   1939
St. Louis Blues   1939
Paradise in Harlem   1939
Stand Up and Fight   1939

Double Deal   1938
Nothing Sacred   1938
Mystery in Swing   1938
A Nation Aflame   1938
Jezebel   1938
One Mile from Heaven   1938
White Bondage   1938

They Won't Forget   1937
Green Pastures   1937

The Black Legion   1937
Penrod and Sam   1937
Slave Ship   1937
Spirit of Youth   1937
Legion of Terror   1937

The Petrified Forest   1936
Fury   1936
Captain Blood   1936

*Public Hero Number
  One*   1935
Helldorado   1935
Imitation of Life   1935
Ouanga   1935

The Cabin in the Cotton   1933
Hypnotized   1933
The Emperor Jones   1933

The Black King   1932
East of Borneo   1932

BLACK FILMS OF THE TWENTIES

Hallelujah   1929
Black Waters   1929
Hearts in Dixie   1929
Melancholy Dame   1929

Uncle Tom's Cabin   1927

*The Florian Slappey
  Series*   1925-26

Broken Chains   1924
Free and Equal   1924

Robinson Crusoe   1923

One Exciting Night   1922

*Ten Nights in a
  Bar-Room*   1920

BLACK FILMS OF THE TEENS

The Our Gang Comedies

*The Greatest Thing
  in Life*   1918

Uncle Tom's Cabin   1918

American Aristocracy   1916

The Nigger   1915
The Coward   1915
The Birth of a Nation   1915

The Wages of Sin   1914
The Broken Violin   1914
Dark Town Jubilee   1914
Coon Town Suffragettes   1914

Uncle Tom's Cabin   1913
*The Battle of Elderbush
  Gulch*   1913
The Octoroon   1913
In Slavery Days   1913

BLACK FILMS OF THE TEENS Continued

Billy's Stratagem   1912
The Debt   1912

The Judge's Story   1911
The Dark Romance of a
   Tobacco Can   1911
For Massa's Sake   1911
The Battle   1910

A Child's Stratagem   1910
The House with Closed
   Shutters   1910
The Thread of Destiny   1910
The Honour of his
   Family   1910

EARLY BLACK FILMS

The Rastus Series   1910

The Sambo Series   1909
The Slave   1909

The Masher   1907

Fights of a Nation   1905
The Wooing and Wedding
   of a Coon   1905

REPRESENTATIVE BLACK DIRECTORS

William Crain
Herbert Danska
Ossie Davis
Ivan Dixon
Wendell James Franklin
Al Freeman, Jr.
Robert L. Goodwin
William Greaves
Bill Gunn
Yaphet Kotto
Stan Lathan
Gil Moses
Roger Moseley

Ron O'Neal
Gordon Parks
Gordon Parks, Jr.
Sidney Poitier
Hugh A. Robertson
Michael A. Schultz
Mel Stewart
Raymond St. Jacques
Christopher St. John
Melvin Van Peebles
Mark Warren
Oscar Williams

REPRESENTATIVE BLACK PRODUCERS

Pervis Atkins
Harry Belafonte
Bill Cosby
Sammy Davis, Jr.
Ivan Dixon
Robert L. Goodwin
Berry Gordy, Jr.
Joe Hartsfield
Forest Hamilton
Sam Greenlee

Horace Jackson
Jack Jordan
Max Julian
Tony King
Woody King
Yaphet Kotto
Tony Major
Gordon Parks
Brock Peters
Sidney Poitier

REPRESENTATIVE BLACK PRODUCERS Continued

Matty Robinson
Larry Shaw
Raymond St. Jacques
Christopher St. John

Melvin Van Peebles
Oscar Williams
Fred Williamson

REPRESENTATIVE BLACK SCREENWRITERS

Maya Angelou
William Branch
Ron Cutler
Ossie Davis
George Davis
Ruby Dee
Lonne Elder III
J. E. Franklin
Joe Green

Sam Greenlee
Bill Gunn
Alex Haley
Lorraine Hansberry
Horace Jackson
Robert L. Goodwin
John Killens
Woodie King
Julian Mayfield

Tony Major
Gordon Parks
Richard Pryor
Louis Peterson
Christopher St. John
Melvin Van Peebles
Drake Walker
Joseph A. Walker
Don Williams

REPRESENTATIVE BLACK SCORERS

Gil Askey
Maya Angelou
Roy Ayers
James Brown
Solomon Burke
Jerry Butler
Bill Cosby
Marvin Gaye
Herbie Hancock

Donny Hathaway
Isaac Hayes
Willie Hutch
J. J. Johnson
Booker T. Jones
Quincy Jones
Taj Mahal
Tom McIntosh
Curtis Mayfield

Obisiba
Gordon Parks
Johnny Pate
Billy Preston
Joe Simon
Melvin Van Peebles
Sam Waymon
Barry White
Bobby Womack

REPRESENTATIVE BLACK FILM PRODUCTION COMPANIES

American Black Star Productions
Bokari Ltd.
Chamba Productions
Chocolate Chip Productions
Denmara Productions
E & R Productions
Harlem Audio Visual
Harry Belafonte Productions
Jemmin Productions
Jymie Productions
K-Calb Productions
Kelly-Jordan Enterprises
Motown Productions

New Era Communications
Reels and Reality
Robert L. Goodwin Productions
Sepia Productions
Shaka Productions
St. Jacques Productions
Trans-Oceanic Productions
Third World Cinema
Uniworld Films, Inc.
William Greaves Productions
William Tenant Productions
Verdon Production Company
Yeah Inc.

REPRESENTATIVE EARLY BLACK FILM
PRODUCTION COMPANIES

The Birth of a Race Company
Coloured Players Film
  Corporation
Ebony Films

Gate City Film Corporation
Lincoln Motion Picture
  Company
Renaissance Films

ACADEMY AWARD NOMINATIONS

1972	Sidney J. Furie	*Lady Sings the Blues*	Best Film
1972	Diana Ross	*Lady Sings the Blues*	Best Actress
1972	Gil Askey	*Lady Sings the Blues*	Best Score
1972	Terence McCloy	*Lady Sings the Blues*	Best Script
1972	Elizabeth Courtney	*Lady Sings the Blues*	Best Costumes
1972	Robert B. Radnitz	*Sounder*	Best Film
1972	Cicely Tyson	*Sounder*	Best Actress
1972	Paul Winfield	*Sounder*	Best Actor
1972	Lonne Elder III	*Sounder*	Best Screenplay
1972	Marvin Worth Arnold Perl	*Malcolm X*	Best Documentary
1971	Isaac Hayes	*Shaft*	Best Score
1971	Isaac Hayes*	*Shaft*	Best Theme Song
1970	James Earl Jones	*The Great White Hope*	Best Actor
1970	Rupert Crosse	*The Reivers*	Best Supporting Actor
1970	Ely Landau	*King: From Montgomery to Memphis*	Best Documentary
1969	Quincey Jones	*In Cold Blood*	Best Score
1969	Hugh A. Robertson	*Midnight Cowboy*	Best Film Editing
1968	Quincey Jones	*For Love of Ivy*	Best Theme Song
1967	Quincey Jones	*Banning*	Best Theme Song
1967	Beah Richards	*Guess Who's Coming to Dinner*	Best Supporting Actress
1963	Sidney Poitier*	*Lilies of the Field*	Best Actor
1959	Breno Mello	*Black Orpheus*	Best Foreign Film
1959	Juanita Moore	*Imitation of Life*	Best Supporting Actress
1958	Sidney Poitier	*The Defiant Ones*	Best Actor
1954	Dorothy Dandridge	*Carmen Jones*	Best Actress
1947	James Baskette	*Song of the South*	Special Award
1939	Hattie McDaniel*	*Gone with the Wind*	Best Supporting Actress

*Award Winners. Academy Awards were first given in 1927.

Index

DATE			